READY

TO

RETURN

Bringing Back the Church's Lost Generation

Ken Ham with Jeff Kinley

research by Britt Beemer

First printing: August 2015

Master Books®, P.O. Box 726, Green Forest, AR 72638
Master Books® is a division of the New Leaf Publishing Group, Inc.

ISBN: 978-0-89051-836-6
Library of Congress Number: 2015947460
Cover by Diana Bogardus

Unless otherwise noted, Scripture quotations are from The Holy Bible, English Standard Version Copyright © 2001 by Crossway Bibles, a publishing ministry of Good News Publishers.
Scripture quotations marked KJV are taken from the King James Version.

Scripture quotations marked NKJV are taken from the New King James Version®. Copyright © 1982 by Thomas Nelson. Used by permission. All rights reserved.

Scripture quotations marked NIV are taken from the Holy Bible, New International Version®, NIV® Copyright ©1973, 1978, 1984, 2011 by Biblica, Inc.® Used by permission. All rights reserved worldwide.

Scripture quotations marked NASB are taken from the New American Standard Bible Copyright © 1960, 1962, 1963, 1968, 1971, 1972, 1973, 1975, 1977, 1995 by The Lockman FoundationPlease consider requesting that a copy of this volume be purchased by your local library system.

Printed in the United States of America

Please visit our website for other great titles:
www.masterbooks.com

For information regarding author interviews,
please contact the publicity department at (870) 438-5288.

Master
Books®
A Division of New Leaf Publishing Group
www.masterbooks.com

Dedication

As this book is about the younger generations who will be the leaders in the culture in the future, I dedicate this book to our 14 grandchildren:

Malachi, Kathryn, Noah, Kylie, Caleb, Lacey, Madelyn, Nicole, Emma, Josiah, Lexie, Kendra, Amelia, Olivia. May God mightily use godly offspring as these to call Church and culture back to the authority of the Word of God.

— Ken Ham, President of Answers in Genesis

Parent Dedication

Having great parents is worth more than all the gold at Ft. Knox!

My parents, Elvin and Margaret Beemer gave me freedom to experience the world at a young age by allowing me to work on Capitol Hill through my high school, college and graduate school days. My father taught "he would rather see a sermon than hear one." My mother lovingly pushed me to do mighty things such as starting ARG with little capital.

My wife's parents, Tom and Catie Cook, represent the most perfect, loving couple who are so gentle to one another that their undying love for each other oozes out of them for all the world to see.

These two couple come from different backgrounds, but help me to better understand love.

— Britt Beemer, America's Research Group

Contents

Chapter 1

A Call to Reformation

On October 31, 1517, a German priest nailed a sheet of paper to a Catholic Church door in Wittenburg, Germany. Little did he know in doing so that his protest would change the world. But it wasn't so much his act of defiance that got people's attention as what was written on that particular piece of paper. Long concerned and dissatisfied with the state of Christianity in his day, Martin Luther's now immortal "95 Theses" itemized serious grievances he had against the Church he loved and served. He had originally intended his objections to be used as points of discussion, calling the corporate church institution back toward more biblical understanding beliefs and practices.

Instead, what it got him was excommunicated.

And with that, Protestantism was born.

As with many other organizations, the Church tends to drift and fade over time, losing her original simplicity, passion, and purpose. Without strong leadership and a constant calibration back to her primary calling, the Bride that Jesus courted is in danger of losing her very identity.

But it's not so much that we need another Martin Luther. No, instead we need an entire generation of Luthers! We are in desperate need of Christians who are not content to allow the church drift, disconnected from the anchor of God's truth. Tossed back and forth by every wind and wave of doctrine, and without a clear course to guide her, she is in peril, susceptible to imminent shipwreck or sinking. And those on board are destined to drown in a sea of ignorance, impotence, uncertainty, and ineffectiveness.

And nothing would grieve God's heart more than this.

From a human perspective, the Western Church appears to be in big trouble. Any astute observer can see that the culture of the Church is becoming more secularized with each passing day. And in this book, we are detailing new research on the Church that will reveal distressing trends — and particularly with millennials. In many ways, even the leadership of the Church has adopted many of the world's beliefs and teachings. As a result, Jesus' Bride does not influence the culture as it once did. On the contrary, this book will demonstrate how the culture is influencing the Church in critical areas. But what often goes unnoticed is the damage that has been done in the hearts and minds of coming generations. The latest research conducted by America's Research Group reveals shocking realities concerning the state of the evangelical Church in America — a picture of what is happening through the Western world. And the looming question is, "Where will the Church be in the next generation?" The research is very eye opening, and provides a grave warning for the Church and its leaders. The results of our research should also alert every parent, as it reveals where their children and the next generation already are, spiritually speaking. This generation of millennials will fundamentally change the culture, unless they return to a truly biblical foundation. But this is also a call to action for Christians in this millennial demographic.

The Bible makes it clear that the true Church is made up of the body of believers throughout the world. Even so, we continue to struggle and drift because of our inherent bent toward sin. As Paul wrote,

> . . . but I see in my members another law waging war against the law of my mind and making me captive to the law of sin that dwells in my members. Wretched man that I am! Who will deliver me from this body of death? Thanks be to God through Jesus Christ our Lord! So then, I myself serve the law of God

with my mind, but with my flesh I serve the law of sin (Rom. 7:23–25).

And yet, even as believers struggle, the Lord Jesus Christ nevertheless declared,

> I will build my church, and the gates of hell shall not prevail against it (Matt. 16:18).

Paul's words to the Philippians echo this truth for the Church:

> And I am sure of this, that he who began a good work in you will bring it to completion at the day of Jesus Christ (Phil. 1:6).

These two oppositional truths — our struggle with sin and Jesus' commitment to build His Church and to bring believers to maturity — both co-exist, though admittedly with great tension at times. So while Christians contend with sin, the Church itself is still being built by Jesus, moving forward by His sovereign decree.

In the book *Already Gone*, we discussed why there's an exodus of coming generations from the church.[1] We featured photographs of church buildings in England that were no longer being used for Christians to gather in to worship and hear the teaching of the Word of God. Instead, these buildings have been transformed into music stores, nightclubs, museums, etc. But the buildings themselves are not the issue. What's even more tragic is that the exodus from the church's facilities is but a physical picture of the spiritual departure across the United Kingdom, and actually across all of Europe. Today, only a small percentage of Europeans attend any type of church, with most identifying as having no religious affiliation at all. Such a phenomenon is on the rise here in the USA as well. What is happening in Europe is a picture of where the USA will be in the future if the spiritual state of coming generations is not changed.

Of course, God's Word does not promise that a particular local church will necessarily continue in existence. However, the Church universal *will* continue as long as the church age endures. God will preserve

---

1. Ken Ham and Britt Beemer, *Already Gone* (Green Forest, AR: Master Books, 2009).

His Church (those who are redeemed by the blood of the lamb) and its work in this world (the preaching of the gospel). This, despite the fact that "we wrestle not against flesh and blood, but against principalities, against powers, against the rulers of the darkness of this world, against spiritual wickedness in high places" (Eph. 6:12; KJV).

Yes, God will preserve His Church. No principality or power will ever be able to stop His work, halt the preaching of the gospel, demolish His Church in general, or ruin any particular soul that is built upon the rock that is Christ.

At the same time, this does not mean there will not be great failings within the Church, just as we saw great failings with God's people in the Old Testament and in the Middle Ages.

Uncompromising Faith

Our latest research reminds me of the ministry of two great men in the Old Testament. The first is the prophet Jeremiah, who warned people about God's judgment because of rampant compromise. The second is King Hezekiah, who was prepared to bring very needed reforms.

Many failings of God's people are recorded in the Old Testament, but there are three in particular I want to bring to your attention. They're summarized through the Word of the Lord given to Jeremiah and what happened in Hezekiah's day:

> 1. God's people had not been influencing the world for the Lord God as they were instructed to do by His Word, but instead were learning the ways of the pagan world. As Jeremiah reminded the people: "Learn not the way of the nations . . ." (Jer. 10:2).
>
> 2. Having been influenced by pagan gods and the rampant idolatry of the time, Israel had not stood uncompromisingly for their Creator-God. Instead, she ignored His Word while pursuing contemporary pagan practices. Jeremiah's words then became a scathing rebuke: "But the LORD is the true God; he is the living God and the everlasting King. At his wrath the earth quakes, and the nations cannot endure his indignation. Thus shall you say to them: 'The gods who did not make the heavens

and the earth shall perish from the earth and from under the heavens' " (Jer. 10:10–11).

The third way Israel had failed was that,

> 3. The shepherds (the religious leaders) were leading people astray: "For the shepherds are stupid and do not inquire of the LORD; therefore they have not prospered, and all their flock is scattered" (Jer. 10:21).

As I read Jeremiah 10, I couldn't help but apply this to the Western Church today as I thought about the results of this latest research. Please read it and decide for yourself:

> Hear the word which the LORD speaks to you, O house of Israel. Thus says the LORD:
>
> "Do not learn the way of the Gentiles; do not be dismayed at the signs of heaven, for the Gentiles are dismayed at them. For the customs of the peoples are futile; for one cuts a tree from the forest, the work of the hands of the workman, with the ax. They decorate it with silver and gold; they fasten it with nails and hammers so that it will not topple. They are upright, like a palm tree, and they cannot speak; they must be carried, because they cannot go by themselves. Do not be afraid of them, for they cannot do evil, nor can they do any good."
>
> Inasmuch as there is none like You, O LORD (You are great, and Your name is great in might), who would not fear You, O King of the nations? For this is Your rightful due. For among all the wise men of the nations, and in all their kingdoms, there is none like You. But they are altogether dull-hearted and foolish; a wooden idol is a worthless doctrine. Silver is beaten into plates; it is brought from Tarshish, and gold from Uphaz, the work of the craftsman and of the hands of the metalsmith; blue and purple are their clothing; they are all the work of skillful men. But the LORD is the true God; He is the living God and the everlasting King. At His wrath the earth will tremble, and the nations will not be able to endure His indignation.

Thus you shall say to them: "The gods that have not made the heavens and the earth shall perish from the earth and from under these heavens." He has made the earth by His power, He has established the world by His wisdom, and has stretched out the heavens at His discretion. When He utters His voice, there is a multitude of waters in the heavens: "And He causes the vapors to ascend from the ends of the earth. He makes lightning for the rain, He brings the wind out of His treasuries." Everyone is dull-hearted, without knowledge; every metalsmith is put to shame by an image; for his molded image is falsehood, and there is no breath in them. They are futile, a work of errors; in the time of their punishment they shall perish. The Portion of Jacob is not like them, for He is the Maker of all things, and Israel is the tribe of His inheritance; the LORD of hosts is His name. Gather up your wares from the land, O inhabitant of the fortress!

For thus says the LORD: "Behold, I will throw out at this time the inhabitants of the land, and will distress them, that they may find it so." Woe is me for my hurt! My wound is severe. But I say, "Truly this is an infirmity, and I must bear it." My tent is plundered, and all my cords are broken; my children have gone from me, and they are no more. There is no one to pitch my tent anymore, or set up my curtains. For the shepherds have become dull-hearted, and have not sought the LORD; therefore they shall not prosper, and all their flocks shall be scattered. Behold, the noise of the report has come, and a great commotion out of the north country, to make the cities of Judah desolate, a den of jackals. O LORD, I know the way of man is not in himself; it is not in man who walks to direct his own steps. O LORD, correct me, but with justice; not in Your anger, lest You bring me to nothing. Pour out Your fury on the Gentiles, who do not know You, and on the families who do not call on Your name; for they have eaten up Jacob, devoured him and consumed him, and made his dwelling place desolate (Jer. 10:1–25; NKJV).

As you look at the culture we're in, can you see how we too have forgotten God and replaced Him with our own idols? Jeremiah laments the desolation of his people while at the same time warning them of God's impending judgment. In her brief history, America was once a nation heavily influenced by the Church and biblical principles. However, the latest research on the Church we are detailing in this book shows that, across the denominations, the modern Church,

    1. Is not influencing the culture as it once did, because many aspects of secular culture have infiltrated the Church.

    2. So much of the Church has adopted the pagan religion of the day and compromised God's Word.

    3. The majority of Church leaders have been leading the people astray by not teaching God's Word as they should, and by not preparing the Church to be equipped to defend the faith.

At the same time, it's important to understand that there is a remnant among God's people and among Church leaders. Like Elijah, they're fully standing on God's Word against the "prophets of Baal." This remnant reminds us that God's work can never be thwarted (Job 42:2).

I pray these findings will be a wakeup call to the Church. After considering this research in detail, my heart is burdened because of the sad state of Christianity today. But I am also encouraged because I know that with God's enablement, Bible-believing Christians can turn things around. The task seems so impossibly great, and the challenges overwhelming. But our God is greater!

Being "On Mission"

As I was recently rereading our ministry's mission statement, the Lord brought something to my mind that should encourage every believer who is burdened to reach this world with the gospel.

Our ministry's official goal at Answers in Genesis is "to support the church in fulfilling its commission." To accomplish this goal, our "vision statement" reads, "Answers in Genesis is a catalyst to bring reformation by reclaiming the foundations of our faith which are found in the Bible, from the very first verse."

This comprehensive vision includes our,

Mission

- We proclaim the absolute truth and authority of the Bible with boldness.

- We relate the relevance of a literal Genesis to the Church and the world today with creativity.

- We obey God's call to deliver the message of the gospel, individually and collectively.

Core Values

- We resourcefully equip believers to defend their faith with excellence.

- We willingly engage society's challenges with uncompromising integrity.

- We sacrificially serve the AiG family and others.

- We generously give Christian love.

Note that our vision involves "to bring reformation."[2] When we think of the word *reformation*, Christians usually think of the great reformer Martin Luther whom I spoke of at the beginning of this chapter. However, long before Martin Luther, Scripture gives examples of other key reformers from whom we can learn many lessons. One of the most valuable examples is that of King Hezekiah. God made sure details about his life and reforms would be written down in His holy Word, so we could learn from his actions and be challenged in our own walk of faith.

Concerning the magnitude of Hezekiah's amazing reforms, the Bible says, "So there was great joy in Jerusalem, for since the time of Solomon the son of David, king of Israel, there had been nothing like this in Jerusalem" (2 Chron. 30:26).

---

2. You can read our full Vision/Mission/Core Beliefs Statement online. It tells more about what drives this ministry, but for our purpose here let me focus on the "Vision" portion.

Hezekiah reformed God's people by destroying idol worship and restoring temple worship. He reinstituted the Passover, and did whatever he could and needed to do to get people back to obeying His Word.

We need a "Hezekiah-style happening" in our own culture today. As our research shows, so many believers in our generation have compromised God's Word, beginning in Genesis! We are also seeing the sad consequences (abortion on demand, gay "marriage," increasing violence, etc.) of a Western world that is becoming increasingly more anti-Christian, and attempting to remove any vestiges of Christian influence and heritage from these nations.

So what are the lessons we can learn from Hezekiah?

1. Reformation begins with us

What was different about Hezekiah compared to so many of the other kings of Israel and Judah who came before him? At the beginning of 2 Chronicles' account of Hezekiah we read: "And he did what was right in the eyes of the LORD, according to all that David his father had done" (2 Chron. 29:2).

In addition to his reforms, Hezekiah was also a man of godly character:

> Thus Hezekiah did throughout all Judah, and he did what was good and right and true before the LORD his God. And every work that he undertook in the service of the house of God and in accordance with the law and the commandments, seeking his God, he did with all his heart, and prospered" (2 Chron. 31:20–21).

So what's the lesson? In order to impact the world around them, God's people first need to seek God and be obedient to His Word. Sadly, so many Christians and Christian leaders today exalt *man's* word (like swallowing the lie of evolutionary biology, geology, astronomy, anthropology, etc., which is an attempt to explain life *without* God) and by twisting God's infallible Word to fit that false narrative (theistic evolution). This is no different from the efforts by the people of Judah and Israel to adopt the pagan religion of their age and mix it with what God had instructed.

Reformation begins with a return to the authority of the Word of God and obeying God's revelation to man. By returning to God's Word, beginning in Genesis, and by repenting of the rampant compromise that has spread throughout the Church and Christian institutions, we can reform the failing Church.

2. We should expect resistance and opposition

We read about some of Hezekiah's specific initiatives in 2 Chronicles 30:1 and 30:5:

> Hezekiah sent to all Israel and Judah, and wrote letters also to Ephraim and Manasseh, that they should come to the house of the LORD at Jerusalem, to keep the Passover to the LORD, the God of Israel. . . . So they decreed to make a proclamation throughout all Israel, from Beersheba to Dan, that the people should come and keep the Passover to the LORD, the God of Israel, at Jerusalem, for they had not kept it as often as prescribed.

However, this return to obedience was not enthusiastically received by everyone.

> So the couriers went from city to city through the country of Ephraim and Manasseh, and as far as Zebulun, but they laughed them to scorn and mocked them (2 Chron. 30:10).

As Hezekiah was calling on people to "return to the Lord" (2 Chronicles 30:9), many scoffed. The same is true today, reminding anyone who shares the Word faithfully that there will be those who oppose and ridicule such faithfulness. In fact, we should *expect* scoffers. However, we also read, "However, some men of Asher, of Manasseh, and of Zebulun humbled themselves and came to Jerusalem" (2 Chron. 30:11). God had a remnant that were committed to do what was right before the Lord. And there is a remnant today in our Western cultures. As I travel across the USA and meet people visiting the Creation Museum, I am encouraged at the remnant who are faithful to the Lord and His Word, and who are training up generations to boldly and uncompromisingly stand on the authority of the Word. They are a remnant (and I see them as a growing remnant in the USA), amidst a world of scoffers.

Presumably, nearly everyone scoffed at Noah for preaching God's Word before the Flood came. In 2 Peter 3, we are warned that the most basic teachings of God's Word will be mocked and ridiculed, including the truth about creation, the Flood, and Christ's Second Coming and judgment by fire.

Peter, writing under the inspiration of the Holy Spirit, records,

> Knowing this first, that there shall come in the last days scoffers, walking after to their own lusts, and saying, Where is the promise of His coming? For since the fathers fell asleep, all things continue as they were from the beginning of the creation. For this they willfully are ignorant of, that by the word of God the heavens were of old, and the earth standing out of the water and in the water: whereby the world that then was, being over-flowed with water, perished (2 Pet. 3:3–6; KJV).

Clearly, many in our world today ridicule and repudiate those who stand on God's Word in Genesis and reject man's beliefs concerning the supposed big bang, billions of years, and other evolutionary ideas. As Answers in Genesis moved forward with the construction of a life-size ark, we experienced this same type of scoffing, and it has only increased with time. So if we are staying true to God's Word and we "contend for the faith" (Jude 1:3), we will be mocked, ridiculed, and even persecuted, as Jesus predicted in John 15:18–21.

3. Religious leaders often compromise

There's an interesting contrast in 2 Chronicles 29:34 between the priests (the religious leaders) and the common Levites (those who assisted them).

> But the priests were too few and could not flay all the burnt offerings, so until other priests had consecrated themselves, their brothers the Levites helped them, until the work was finished — for the Levites were more upright in heart than the priests in consecrating themselves.

Throughout the Old and New Testaments, we're warned of shepherds (religious leaders) who lead the people astray. This is certainly not true of all leaders — but even in our world today, we find a large number of Church leaders compromise God's Word as it relates to Genesis or other areas of morality (e.g., homosexuality). Some prefer not to preach tough topics (like sin, repentance, and hell) for fear of upsetting people, especially those who make significant financial contributions.

In 2006, Answers in Genesis contracted with America's Research Group to conduct research on the state of Christian colleges in the USA. The results were published in our book *Already Compromised*.[3] One of the surprising results of that research showed that, by and large, the *science* departments at Christian colleges were more likely to believe in a young earth and reject other evolutionary ideas than the *Bible* (or theology) departments!

It confirmed one of the observations I've made over the past 30-plus years in creation apologetics: even in the more conservative Christian colleges, the professors in the science departments tend to be much more vocal and diligent than Bible departments in dealing with the issue of origins and taking a stand on a literal interpretation of Genesis!

So today, we experience the same problems with our religious leaders that Israel did thousands of years ago. It's true that the heart of the human problem is that of the human heart. It remains deceitful and diseased (Jer. 17:9).

4. Pride threatens us all

Now here is a very serious warning for all of us! The problem of pride. Even as great a man of God as Hezekiah was, his pride nevertheless got the best of him. At first, he was humble and God greatly blessed his faith. After the many reforms Hezekiah performed, God allowed the king of Assyria to come against Judah and intended on war against Jerusalem. Hezekiah fortified the city, made weapons, and prepared for the battle. But most importantly, he encouraged the people to trust in God, who was on their side:

---

3. Ken Ham and Greg Hall, *Already Compromised* (Green Forest, AR: Master Books, 2011).

"Be strong and courageous. Do not be afraid or dismayed before the king of Assyria and all the horde that is with him, for there are more with us than with him. With him is an arm of flesh, but with us is the LORD our God, to help us and to fight our battles." And the people took confidence from the words of Hezekiah king of Judah (2 Chron. 32:7–8).

When the king of Assyria sent people to taunt the Jews and mock their God, Hezekiah did what we should all do for every challenge, every day: "And for this cause Hezekiah the king, and the prophet Isaiah the son of Amoz, *prayed and cried to heaven*" (2 Chron. 32:20; KJV, emphasis added).

Because of this, God gave Hezekiah great victory, and I find it thrilling every time I read it:

And the LORD sent an angel, who cut off all the mighty warriors and commanders and officers in the camp of the king of Assyria. So he returned with shame of face to his own land. And when he came into the house of his god, some of his own sons struck him down there with the sword. So the LORD saved Hezekiah and the inhabitants of Jerusalem from the hand of Sennacherib king of Assyria and from the hand of all his enemies, and he provided for them on every side (2 Chron. 32:21–22).

What a great victory for the Lord!

But now comes the lesson every one of us must learn. Scripture warns us about pride. Because of our sin nature, this is a problem we all have. After the great victory God gave Hezekiah, we read these sad words:

In those days Hezekiah became sick and was at the point of death, and he prayed to the LORD, and he answered him and gave him a sign. But Hezekiah did not make return according to the benefit done to him, for his heart was proud. Therefore wrath came upon him and Judah and Jerusalem (2 Chron. 32:24–25).

Because of the wonderful defeat of the Assyrian army, Hezekiah became proud! When we are involved in serving the Lord, no matter how great or small, we must always remember to give God the glory and honor. We must recognize how easy it is to be lifted up in pride and thus set the wrong example for those looking at us.

This episode could have been his downfall, but then "Hezekiah humbled himself for the pride of his heart, both he and the inhabitants of Jerusalem, so that the wrath of the LORD did not come upon them in the days of Hezekiah" (2 Chron. 32:26).

We can never forget that Satan's greatest temptations often come immediately on the heels of a great victory. It is typically then that our guard is down and we are most vulnerable to attack and to the deceptive nature of human pride. Solomon reminds us,

> One's pride will bring him low, but he who is lowly in spirit will obtain honor (Prov. 29:23).

5. A lasting legacy requires vigilance

There is one final lesson I want to highlight in Hezekiah's reformation story. When Hezekiah died, we read that his son Manasseh became king in his place. But then "[Manassah] did what was evil in the sight of the LORD, according to the abominations of the nations whom the LORD drove out before the people of Israel" (2 Chron. 33:2).

It is hard to fathom how such a godly king as Hezekiah could end up with such an evil son as Manasseh to take his place. We don't know the circumstances of why Manasseh ended up the way he did. But it underscores the fact that every generation must choose for itself to follow the Lord. It's also a warning to us that we must always be vigilant and do the very best we can to raise up offspring who will carry on the spiritual legacy to the next generation and then the next and so on.

It's sad to observe that as compromise has crept in, many Christian institutions (colleges, etc.) in our Western world have forsaken the biblical stand of our nation's founders. Ironically, many such institutions, established on biblical principles, have now become leaders in indoctrinating generations *against* the authority of the Word of God. This is tragic and unacceptable.

Charles Spurgeon, the great Baptist preacher who brought revival to his native Britain, proclaimed,

We want again Luthers, Calvins, Bunyans, Whitefields, men fit to mark eras, whose names breathe terror in our foe-men's ears. We have dire need of such. Whence will they come to us? They are the gifts of Jesus Christ to the Church, and will come in due time. He has power to give us back again a golden age of preachers, and when the good old truth is once more preached by men whose lips are touched as with a live coal from off the altar, this shall be the instrument in the hand of the Spirit for bringing about a great and thorough revival of religion in the land. . . . I do not look for any other means of converting men beyond the simple preaching of the gospel and the opening of men's ears to hear it. The moment the Church of God shall despise the pulpit, God will despise her. It has been through the ministry that the Lord has always been pleased to revive and bless His Churches.[4]

Yes, we need Luthers and Hezekiah-type reformers today. But we must understand and embrace the sober lessons from the life of Jeremiah (in warning the people) and Hezekiah's (in bringing needed reforms), which God put in His Word for our good. We must return to God's infallible Word, and pursue the true reform that rests in Him alone.

---

4. Charles Spurgeon, *Autobiography Vol. 1: The Early Years* (Edinburth, UK: Banner of Truth, 1973).

Chapter 2

The State of the Modern Church

Christendom in Decline

F ew Americans are aware of the spiritual epidemic that wiped out the land of our Christian forefathers. Even fewer are aware that the same epidemic has reached our own shores, spreading like a virus.

In 2009, I attended Sunday services at an impressive 19th-century church in London. In a building with seating for 3,000 in ornate pews, a handful of elderly people sat inside . . . in chairs set up in the foyer.

The service, held in a vibrant city full of millions of people, reminded me of a funeral — not the funeral of a person, but the funeral of a once-great institution. In the past 40+ years, 1,600 churches in England, with hundreds of years of ministry behind them, have shut their doors, according to an architectural preservation group called the Victorian Society.

Today, few Americans are aware of the spiritual epidemic that devastated the land of our Christian forefathers. Even fewer are aware that the same epidemic has reached our own shores, spreading like a virus.

American Christianity could in a sense become almost extinct in less than two generations — if Christians in this country don't act quickly and decisively. Respected pollster George Barna was one of the first to put numbers to this epidemic, finding that six out of ten 20-somethings who were involved in a church during their teen years are already gone. Since that research was published in 2000, survey after survey has confirmed the same basic trend. Many of the 20s generation are leaving the Church in droves with few returning.

Young people see through the hypocrisy of those who claim to believe the Bible — just not as it's written. And when they do, they leave both the Church *and* their trust in God's Word behind. Hear what we have to say in the revealing book *Already Gone*.

In 2009, the book *Already Gone* (co-authored by myself and researcher Britt Beemer) was published, detailing the results of what we believe to be the first scientific study of its kind on the 20s generation, which was conducted by respected Americas Research Group led by CEO Britt Beemer. The "Beemer Report" reveals startling facts discovered through 20,000 phone calls and detailed surveys of a thousand 20–29-year-olds who used to attend evangelical churches on a regular basis, but have since left it behind.

The results were shocking:

- Those who faithfully attend Sunday school are more likely to leave the Church than those who do not.

- Those who regularly attended Sunday school are more likely to believe that the Bible is less true.

- Those who regularly attended Sunday school are actually more likely to defend that abortion and gay marriage should be legal.

- Those who regularly attended Sunday school are actually more likely to defend premarital sex.

The authors challenged the Church to deal with this issue before we lose coming generations!

The problem, in both the United Kingdom and America, began when the Church basically disconnected the Bible from the real world. Churches in America are not places where people typically talk about dinosaurs, fossils, or the age of the earth — that is left up to the secular schools and colleges. Effectively, the Church concentrates on the spiritual and moral aspects of Christianity.

But the Bible is not some "pie in the sky" theoretical book. It's a real book of history connected to the real world. It has everything to do with history, geology, biology, anthropology, and sociology. It provides the true history of the world, as opposed to evolution, whose narrative claims millions of years and naturalism.

The "disconnect" between faith and fact is an illusion created by an overwhelming misinterpretation of the difference between what one can observe versus one's interpretation of facts in regard to the past. Observational science (based on direct observation, the repeatable test etc.), confirms the Bible's history and, thus, also the Christian doctrines (like the gospel) that are based in that history.

As I travel around the world teaching how to defend biblical principles and history, I find that whether my audience is secular or Christian, they ask the same questions, such as,

- How do you know the Bible is true?[1]

- Hasn't science disproved the Bible?[2]

- Isn't the world millions of years old?[3]

- How did Noah get all the animals on the ark?[4]

- But don't we observe evolution because we see animals change — bacteria become resistant to antibiotics?[5]

- How can you believe in a loving God with so much death and suffering in the world?

- Don't dinosaurs disprove the Bible's account of creation in Genesis?

---

1. https://answersingenesis.org/bible/.
2. https://answersingenesis.org/science/.
3. https://answersingenesis.org/age-of-the-earth/.
4. https://answersingenesis.org/noahs-ark/.
5. https://answersingenesis.org/evolution/.

- How can you believe there were only two people to begin with when we have so many different races of people?

Fortunately, there are answers to these and the many other questions people ask today. But sadly, in most churches and homes, those answers have not been taught to coming generations that have become so secularized (much like a "Greek" pagan culture).

Typical churches use resources more geared for what could be called the "Jew in Jerusalem" — someone who has developed a religious background and who lives in a religiously friendly community of faith and understands the terms used.

A Disturbing Trend

But we are now in the era of the "Greeks" — like the secular philosophers the Apostle Paul encountered on Mars Hill. Yet our churches and Sunday schools are still teaching us like Jews.

With our society immersed in secularism, it's essential that we learn how to defend the Bible and the Christian faith in that arena, and to do it for our sake and our children's — for unless we do, the empty and obsolete churches in England will foreshadow the future of Christianity in America.

The Victorian Society's magazine in 2007 carried a headline that read, "Redundant Churches: Who Cares?"[6] Churches in the United Kingdom have been turned into theaters, restaurants, museums — even mosques and temples. I have a whole series of photographs that I have taken of such buildings that were formerly churches.

Where England is today, America will be tomorrow — unless we act now and pray for God's favor.

As stated in the previous chapter, it is time for a new Reformation in the Church — to call the Body of Christ back to the authority of the Word of God, beginning with His first words in Genesis.

As a follow-up to the research detailed in the 2009 publication *Already Gone,* in 2014, Answers in Genesis contracted with America's Research Group (ARG) once again, to understand more about the state of the modern Church and particularly the younger generations. The

---

6. http://www.victoriansociety.org.uk/publications/redundant-churches-who-cares/.

data obtained in this study was by telephone interviews of a qualified sample in the United States. This sample was selected by random digit procedure insuring construction of a probability sample. The survey began on July 23, 2014, and concluded on August 1, 2014.

ARG conducted this research to provide Answers in Genesis a completed study of people in their 20s and 40s who attend church. One of AiG's goals was to determine what exactly has happened to their faith and their church attendance. Specifically, this study investigated the following areas of concern:

- Denomination

- Current church attendance

- Sunday school teaching

- Personal beliefs in biblical accounts

- Church relevance

- Evolution/creation

In this book we will provide and explain various aspects of this research in detail. My hope in doing this is that,

- An alarm bell will be sounded concerning problems with the beliefs of a significant number of people currently attending church — and in particular the 20s generation.

- The meaning of words and terms will be carefully defined and explained in the Church because of the influence of postmodernism. One cannot assume younger generations have the same definitions of terms as previous generations.

- People will gain an understanding of why increasing numbers in the Church are doubting the Scriptures and no longer believing God's Word.

- What should be done in our churches and home to deal with those in the coming generations that are leaving the Church and those who have adopted a very secularized worldview.

- Help wake up Christian leaders and others to see the problems that need to be addressed in the Church and the home, or else the Church's influence will continue to wane in our Western world.

- See clearly that certain Church people will hold biblically contradictory positions and yet not even understand they are doing so.

- People in the Church will develop consistency in how they apply Scripture to their daily lives.

The Research Doesn't Lie

The following is a summary of just some of the highlights of this cutting-edge research to urge you to carefully consider what ARG found.

For instance, of those in their 20s and 40s who attend church,

1. Twenty percent (20.6%) said they don't believe the Bible is true and historically accurate.

2. Twenty-two percent (22.1%) of the people who do not believe the Bible is true and accurate said "the Bible has errors," and that is what made them begin to doubt the Bible.

3. Eighteen percent said their pastor said something to make them believe the Book of Genesis contained many myths and legends.

4. Eighty-three percent said their science teachers taught them that the earth was millions or billions of years old. In addition, 65.2% said their teachers taught them that humans definitely evolved from lower forms of life to become what they are today.

5. Among the 20.6% who do not believe that the Bible is true and historically accurate, 22.1% said the "Bible has errors," while 20.6% said "science shows that the earth is very old," and 20.4% said the "Bible was written by men," stating that this was what made them begin to doubt the Bible. In addition, 13.8% said "the Bible contradicts itself" and 13.4% said their belief that "it hasn't been translated correctly" was that made them begin to doubt the Bible.

6. Only fifty-nine percent said they consider themselves born-again.

7. Forty-two percent who attended Sunday school said their Sunday school teachers did not teach them how to defend their Christian beliefs by reading certain verses in their Bible.

8. Sixty-two percent said they believe if you are a good person on earth, you will go to heaven upon your death.

9. Twenty-three percent (22.9%) said they left high school believing that the Bible is less true. In addition, 28.0% said they feel people with a college education are less likely to attend church.

10. Over seven in ten (72.0%) said they believe the Bible is true and historically accurate. However, 27.0% said they don't believe homosexual behavior is a sin and 30.6% said abortions should continue to be legal in most instances. Thirty-eight percent said they think premarital sex is okay. Two in five said gay couples should be allowed to marry and have all the legal rights of heterosexual couples. Five in nine said homosexual behavior is a sin.

11. Over seven in ten (70+%) said they have not read the Bible from cover to cover.

12. Twenty-two percent (22.4%) said the Bible is a book that many men wrote years ago and it is simply a collection of writings by wise men.

13. Eighty-two percent (82.8%) believe Adam and Eve were real people in the Garden of Eden and 83.6% believe Adam and Eve sinned and were expelled from the Garden. In addition, 73.7% believe in the account of Sodom and Gomorrah and that Lot's wife was turned to salt when she looked back at the city. Further, 89.5% believe in Noah's ark and the global flood and 82.5% believe in the birth of Isaac when Abraham was about 100 years old.

14. Over one in five said they believe other holy books like the Qur'an (Koran) are inspired by God.

15. Of those who do not believe the Bible is true and historically accurate, one in two (50%) said they first had doubts in middle school.

16. Five in nine said they believe that dinosaurs died out before people were on the planet.

17. Two in three said they believe the Bible, which teaches the world was created in six 24-hour days.

18. Less than 50% said someone taught them how to defend their Christian faith if they were challenged.

19. Of those who said no one taught them how to defend their Christian faith, nearly 50% said they would have liked someone to have prepared them better when they were younger on how to defend their faith and Christian principles.

20. Over 20% (one in five) said their pastor taught that Christians could believe in an earth that is millions or billions of years old.

21. One in six said their pastor said something to make them believe that the Book of Genesis contained myths and legends that we now know are untrue.

22. One in three said they currently attend church most Sundays. Nearly one in four said they currently attend church every week. Six in seven said that in elementary school, they primarily attended a public school. Seven in eight said that in high school, they primarily attended a public school.

23. Over one in five said that by the time they graduated from high school, they believed that the Bible was less true. Of those who said that by the time they graduated from high school, they believed that the Bible was less true, five in nine said their high school teacher was the person who convinced them the most that the Bible was less true. Over one in four said the Bible contains errors.

24. Of those who said the Bible contains errors, over one in three said "human writers of the Bible made mistakes" is one of those errors.

25. Fewer than three in five said they believe only those who have received Christ as their Lord and Savior will go to heaven.

26. Seven in eight said science teachers should be allowed to teach the problems with evolution.

27. Six in seven said prayer should be allowed in public schools.

Again, this research was conducted on those who are *attending church*. One in five said they primarily attend a Baptist church (this was the biggest denomination represented). One in nine said they primarily attend a Catholic church. However, when the Catholic denomination was taken out of the groups, the statistics in regard to the answers did not change.

The above summary of the results should in itself generate concern about the state of those attending church today. But it also reveals areas where the Church can (and needs to) address issues to help alleviate these problems. Of course there were some very positive aspects found from the research as well.

As we continue in this book, we will not only provide additional details of this research, but also more importantly give teaching and discuss ways that can be used to address the problems revealed.

As we begin to do this, I believe the first topic we need to address relates to how people in the Church view Scripture itself.

Chapter 3

The Blind and the Bland

The Tragedy of Biblical Devaluation

As we delve into the alarming findings of the latest research on the state of the modern Church, we first need to address the issue of how we view and approach the Bible — the Word of God.

In the ARG survey (of those in their 20s and 40s), we discovered an alarming result indicating that many attending church do not understand what it means to say the Scriptures are the "inspired Word of God."

When asked, "Do you believe all the books of the Bible are inspired by God?" 95 percent answer yes. Now this sounds very encouraging. But the very next question revealed a serious problem. When asked, "Do you believe other holy books are inspired by God?" 22 percent answered yes, and 10 percent didn't know if they were. So to 32 percent of those attending church, God's Word is not just the Bible, but includes or probably includes other books.

The problem in regard to how people in the Church view God's Word is further illustrated when asked "Do you believe the Bible is true and historically accurate?" and 21 percent answered with a no and an additional 7 percent didn't know! We did ask what caused them to answer this way and will deal with that later in the book, but it does relate to a major area of compromise within the church.

When they were asked, "Do you believe God truly inspired each of the authors of books of the Bible?" an encouraging 90 percent answered yes. But when asked, "Does the Bible contain errors?" then 26 percent answered yes, an additional 11 percent didn't know, and 63 percent said no! This means there is a problem in the Church in regard to people understanding what the word "inspired" means. There are obviously different definitions! It's also important to find out then when given the opportunity to express what those errors supposedly are, the largest percentage (37 percent) stated it was that the Bible was wrong about the age of the earth! We will discuss this further on, but there is no doubt the teaching of evolution and "millions of years" has had a dramatic effect on how a significant number of churchgoers view the Bible (let alone those who have already left the Church).

Another glaring problem in regard to how people view Scripture showed up when these churchgoers were asked, "Do you believe if you are a good person you will go to heaven?" An alarming 62 percent answered yes! So even a significant number of those who believe the Bible is the inspired Word of God and don't believe it has errors, believe if you are a good person you will go to heaven! Something is seriously wrong here with their understanding of Scripture! But then, an inconsistency shows up which means there is much confusion. Many people are not thinking through the positions they hold. When asked, "Do you believe only those who have received Christ will go to heaven," 61 percent say yes. Before we go any further into this research, the results certainly show that there is confusion in the Church with the 20s and 40s generations in regard to what it means to say the Bible is the Word of God, specifically the need to interpret it consistently.

One of the major crises in the Church today is that Christian leaders (and Christians in general) have begun to treat God's Holy Word as a fallible *human* work. In other words, they choose to either not take it literally (meaning naturally — the grammatical historical interpretative method), or in some way amend it in order to accommodate a newer, more "enlightened" understanding of the universe, mankind, and truth. Relativism, pluralism, and unorthodox teaching have seeped into many churches, with the most immediate effect being a pandemic biblical illiteracy among church members. This doesn't mean the average churchgoer can't recognize the major accounts from the Bible, but rather that he/she has no basic understanding of the Bible as a whole or the theology it teaches. This sort of theological bankruptcy naturally leads to an outbreak of spiritual anemia. And from there, the Church begins to decay and die. Solomon understood this principle, and thus penned,

> Where there is no prophetic vision the people cast off restraint, but blessed is he who keeps the law (Prov. 29:18).

The idea is that without a clear word from God, the spiritual and moral quality of our lives is directly and severely impacted — thus, "spiritual anemia" and weakness. The result is a vulnerability to attack from our enemies (the world, the flesh, and the devil).

Inevitably, without a high view of Scripture, Christians have no framework of theology or truth about God. Because of our sin nature, left to our own ideas, desires, and the propaganda of culture for our guidance, we end up at the wrong destination.

Why the Bible Is Such a Big Deal

I think it's worth asking, "Why is it so critical that the Bible be the foundation of our thoughts, beliefs, and behavior?" Why not secular society? Government? Philosophy or personal feelings? The first and foremost reason is that the Bible is the only divine book ever written in all of history. Many religions, religious leaders, and philosophers have documented their musings and mandates on paper. But *not one* of them has ever supernaturally *validated* those claims as undeniable truth. Jesus Christ is the only person in history who has certified and substantiated his own claims as well as those of the Old Testament. And He did it in the most unmistakable way, by rising from the dead. Because of this, everything we read in Scripture is not only valid and dependable, but also becomes the ultimate source of truth itself. Paul wanted there to be no doubt as to the divine nature of Scripture and its subsequent effect on us, writing,

> All Scripture is breathed out by God and profitable for teaching, for reproof, for correction, and for training in righteousness, that the man of God may be complete, equipped for every good work (2 Tim. 3:16–17).

So often today, many in the Church treat the Bible as written by mere men —but as we read in 1 Thessalonians 2:13, "For this reason we also constantly thank God that when you received the word of God which you heard from us, you accepted it not as the word of men, but for what it really is, the word of God, which also performs its work in you who believe" (NASB).

The word "inspired" comes from a Greek word meaning "God-breathed." That's how connected Scripture is to God. It's like the very breath of God. His Word, spoken and faithfully recorded on paper for us, reveals His thoughts and the desires of His heart. As such, by its very nature it is perfect, infallible, and most of all, authoritative!

So, given this fact, that authority obviously extends all the way back to the first words in the Bible. Unfortunately, not everyone understands this relationship between God and His Word. Objecting to my strong stand on the six literal days of creation, a pastor once wrote,

> Ham uses deductive reasoning, with only the Bible text as his referent, to make a case for the literal historicity of everything in Scripture. Without such authentication, he claims, the truth of the resurrection is jeopardized. I'm unable to make that jump with him, because to do so would be to make my faith totally dependent on something, i.e., the Bible text historicity, which is, ultimately, a human work.[1]

How tragic that a man who has been tasked by God to declare authoritatively, "Thus says the Lord," treats the Scripture, practically speaking, as a work of *man* (with some divine bits occasionally thrown in).

---

1. Personal letter from a Georgia (USA) pastor on file at AiG-USA.

To be clear, there are conservative Christian scholars who admit that Genesis chapter one, taken on its own, teaches six literal days. However, many of these same Christian leaders, by their own words, were shown to reject the six literal days, because they accepted the billions of years for the age of the earth and universe.[2] This is not only self-contradictory, but is a betrayal of Scripture's very nature and character. It really doesn't require a post-graduate degree in biblical exposition or theology to comprehend that Moses chose the word for "day" (*yom*) in Genesis 1, which when taken in context in accord with the Hebrew language, means a *literal 24-hour day* for each of the days of creation. It follows then that when pastors and teachers cower to evolutionary thought and fallible man-made dating methods used to "reinterpret" what this word means, they end up making God's Word fallible and man's dating methods *in*fallible.[3]

This obviously sets a very dangerous precedent. You can see how, if a typical biblical historical narrative (such as the creation account) doesn't mean what it plainly says and means — then virtually *any* passage in the Bible is up for reinterpretation.[4] Thus, the New Testament would be open to massive reinterpretation and new meanings as well. It makes reading the Bible the same as reading tea leaves at the bottom of a cup — with anyone's interpretation being as valid as anyone else's.

---

2. Ken Ham, "Evolution or Millions of Years — Which Is the Greater Threat?" *Answers Magazine*, July–September 2012; https://answersingenesis.org/theory-of-evolution/millions-of-years/evolution-or-millions-of-years/.
3. Simon Turpin, "Evangelical Commentaries on the Days of Creation in Genesis One," *Answers Research Journal*, 6 (2013): 79–98, https://answersingenesis.org/days-of-creation/evangelical-commentaries-on-the-days-of-creation-in-genesis-one/; also Terry Mortenson, "Six Literal Days," *Answers Magazine*, April–June, 2010, https://answersingenesis.org/days-of-creation/six-literal-days/
4. Some scholars have attempted to reject Genesis as a literal historical account by claiming it was written as poetry. However, this claim is easily refuted: "The Genre of Genesis 1:1–2:3: What Means This Text?" Steven W. Boyd, in *Coming to Grips with Genesis*, Terry Mortenson and Thane Ury, eds. (Green Forest, AR: Master Books, 2008), and https://legacy-cdn-assets.answersingenesis.org/assets/pdf/am/v8/n2/coming-to-grips-with-genesis-ch6.pdf, "Parallelism in Hebrew Poetry Demonstrates a Major Error in the Hermeneutic of Many Old-Earth Creationists," Tim Chaffey, *Answers Research Journal*, 5 (2012): 115–123, https://answersingenesis.org/hermeneutics/parallelism-in-hebrew-poetry-reveals-major-hermaneutic-error/. E.J. Young, in his book *In the Beginning* (Edinburgh: Banner of Truth Trust Publishers, 1976), p. 18, stated: "Hebrew poetry had certain characteristics, and they are not found in the first chapter of Genesis."

Now it is true that Christians can have differing interpretations in regard to issues like eschatology, modes of baptism, and so on. But such differences do not alter the very foundation of history, humanity, or the Christian faith. At least those who disagree about certain non-essential doctrines are still looking at the Bible, interpreting Scripture with Scripture. But the reason so many Christians have differing views of Genesis is because they are starting *outside* of Scripture with man's fallible ideas, and using them to reinterpret the plain meaning of God's Word. In doing so, they force an outside interpretation on God's Word.

Man's Word or God's?

Fortunately, despite man's misinterpretation, God has not left us in the dark when it comes to understanding His Word. For example, in many cases we can understand Old Testament passages through New Testament explanations of them. In other words, very often the Bible interprets itself! Comparing Scripture with Scripture is what is referred to as the "Analogy of Faith."[5]

Paul effectually does this by citing Genesis as actual history in many passages, including Romans 5, 1 Corinthians 15, and Acts 17:26. However, let me show you what happens if you take what God wrote through Paul, reject a literal interpretation of Genesis, and accept a faulty teaching concerning the age of the earth.[6]

The United Kingdom was once a country deeply influenced by Christian thought. However, now it has few vestiges of Christianity left. One of that country's most influential Christian organizations publishes a magazine that includes Sunday school lessons that are used by many

---

5. www.theopedia.com/Analogy_of_faith.
6. The following papers expose the fallibility of radioactive dating methods: "Radiometric Dating: Problems with Assumptions," Andrew Snelling, *Answers Magazine*, October–December, 2009, https://answersingenesis.org/geology/radiometric-dating/radiometric-dating-problems-with-the-assumptions/; Andrew Snelling, "Radioactive 'Dating' Failure," December 1, 1999, https://answersingenesis.org/geology/carbon-14/radioactive-dating-failure/; Andrew Snelling, "U-Th-Pb 'Dating': An Example of False 'Isochrons,'" *Answers in Depth*, December 9, 2009, https://answersingenesis.org/geology/radiometric-dating/u-th-pb-dating-an-example-of-false-isochrons/; A. Snelling, "The Cause of Anomalous Potassium-Argon Ages for Recent Andesite Flows at Mt. Ngauruhoe, New Zealand, and the Implications for Potassium-Argon Dating," *Proceedings of the Fourth International Conference on Creationism*, 1998, p. 503–525.

churches (including many of the more conservative ones) to teach children and adults.[7]

In the March 1998 edition for all ages, we read,

> The study of paleontology has rendered it virtually impossible for a serious scientist to make a case for a six day creation about six thousand years ago, as Christians would once have believed without question.[8]

Of course, the reason most Christians would have "once believed" in a six-day creation "without question" is that this is the obvious and straightforward reading, in context, of Genesis 1, and the understanding of almost 2,000 years of church history and theology.

This prominent Christian magazine was plainly stating that man's study of the fossil record (and his interpretations of it) must now be the standard used to interpret Genesis and the biblical account.

So what then would the person who wrote this Sunday school lesson do with what Paul wrote in the New Testament concerning Genesis?

Further down the same page, the author of this same lesson states:

> Paul clearly believed, as one would expect of a thinker of that era, in a humanity which was descended from a single male — Adam (v. 26). Because at the end of the twentieth century we have access to scientific and literary scholarship that he never had, many would now see that using the Bible as a geological textbook requires it to answer questions in a way that was never intended.

Are you believing this?

There is no doubt that the implication is that because Paul didn't have the fossil and dating research we have today, his writings would

---

7. *Salt: all ages* magazine. The leadership of this organization told us that they do not agree with denigrating those who hold to literal Genesis, (and have taken steps to avoid a repetition). However, they made it clear that in doing so, they are not supporting literal Genesis, and would allow for such views as long ages and theistic evolution. They told us that a correction in *Salt: all ages*, was considered, but decided against. Many historically sound organizations, though many within their ranks are still solid Bible believers, are subject to pressure to "drift" away from the inerrancy of Scripture; this usually starts in Genesis, because of "science."

8. Milton Keynes, *Salt Magazine,* Scripture Union, UK, Jan/Mar 1998 p. 29.

therefore reflect this lack of knowledge and understanding. As a result, we can't really trust what Paul stated concerning origins. After all, he was at a great disadvantage in this area, not being a scientist or enlightened like we are. Poor Paul, all he had was *direct revelation* from Almighty God, the Creator and source of all knowledge!

This cuts to the heart of the Church's problem. It seems most Christians have a gross misunderstanding concerning the nature of divine revelation and the authority of biblical truth. And this can be traced back to a dereliction of duty in the pulpit where pastors propagate such misinterpretations.

But herein lies the core issue: Are the words of Paul (and other authors in the Bible) just human words, reflecting human thoughts and knowledge? If some of the words of Scripture cannot be trusted as accurate, how can we be certain that other parts of Scripture are true? Are only *some* parts of the Bible inspired? Or are some simply "more inspired" than others? And how can we know for sure?

First, let's consider just some of the claims the Bible makes for itself. Over 3,000 times the Bible claims that it is God's Word. As we've already seen from 2 Timothy 3:16, *every word* of Scripture is literally God-breathed. By definition then, they are infallible. Then there are passages such as Psalm 119:160 (KJV), "Thy word is true from the beginning," and verse 89, "Forever, O LORD, thy word is settled in heaven."

Jesus Christ often settled arguments by citing Scripture, which He said "cannot be broken" (John 10:35). Countering Satan's temptations, Jesus repeatedly answered, "It is written" followed by direct quotes from Old Testament Scripture (Matthew 4). Using human logic, if Paul, who lived in a more educated and advanced first century, was misinformed and ignorant concerning truth, how much more misinformed and misguided would the Old Testament writers be? And yet Jesus quoted Moses as His authoritative basis for resisting Satan. How can this be . . . *unless* he believed that *all* Scripture was historically accurate and spiritually trustworthy? You see, if we simply pick and choose which Scriptures are valid and which are not, there remains no ultimate, unchanging standard by which to make such a distinction. Again, interpreting Scripture becomes a "personal thing," a roll of the dice depending on the person. And *we* become the judges of the Bible to see which parts of the book are "believable" to us, based on what secular reasoning dictates. And we also need to remember that concerning Jesus, we read, "In the beginning was the Word, and the Word was with God, and the Word was God" (John 1:1). Jesus is the Word, so every word from Genesis to Revelation is the word of Jesus — not just those in red in the red letter editions of the Bible!

To be clear, some of Scripture's truths and commands were applied to a specific time period, such as O.T. Temple sacrifices, ceremonial cleansings, etc. Even so, there are still timeless *principles* we were meant to learn from those truths. Paul does not discount the truth of the Law of Moses, even though that Law was no longer in effect and applicable because of Jesus' New Covenant (Testament). However, he did point out many contemporary lessons we can still learn from the Law (Rom. 3:19–31; Gal. 2:15–21, 3:10–4:6). But other truths transcend time, flowing seamlessly from age to age and culture to culture. Among these are those truths that speak to the nature of God, man, and the universe. To amend God's truth concerning creation because of new "scientific" discoveries or methods is like declaring mankind to be inherently "good" because of an overwhelming consensus in the modern psychiatric community. This is absurd. When man's opinion contradicts God's clear revelation, we have to stand with God's Word every time. As Paul told the Romans,

> Let God be true though every one were a liar, as it is written, "That you may be justified in your words, and prevail when you are judged" (Rom. 3:4).

The Authority of the Written Word

Even if the entire world's population were to disagree with Scripture, our allegiance remains with God's Word. Noah sure understood this principle. So did Elijah, Daniel, Peter, and John.

The reality is that many in the world and the Church don't like the implications of Scripture's raw theological or historical truths. So they alter and reinterpret them to "fit" a post-modern understanding of the world, life, and themselves. Currently, this is also being done to those Scriptures that claim truth about marriage, sexuality, and morality. But our latest research illustrates how rampant a problem this is in the modern Church — even among those who call themselves "born again."

For Jesus Christ, when Scripture speaks, the Creator speaks (Matt. 19:5). In Matthew 22:23–34, Christ based an argument on resurrection on the tense of a single Old Testament verb. He endorsed the Genesis record of creation (Matt. 19:3–6), as well as Noah's Flood and the ark (Luke 17:26–27). There are hundreds and hundreds of other Scriptures that demonstrate how every word (in the original autographs) is the exact word God wanted there for all people and for all time. And even though God used human authors, He superintended them, so that they recorded without error what He wanted written down (2 Pet. 1:20–21). Throw out this fundamental fact, and we are left with nothing more than another religious book.

Keep in mind, God is infinite in knowledge. *Infinite*. Limitless. No boundaries. That means He has never been hampered by a lack of understanding in geology or astronomy! In fact, He is the reason geology, astronomy, and all science exists. True science always agrees with Scripture. It's man's presuppositions and interpretations of the facts that cause confusion and disagreement. God is not in heaven saying "Okay, I admit it. Paul got it wrong. I sure wish I could have prevented him from writing what more enlightened men will later contradict." Yet that is how an increasing number of people in the Church really view Scripture!

In reality, God actually spoke through Scripture's writers, and He did not stutter, skip a beat, or miss a word. However, because evangelical Christianity is currently suffering from a really low view of Scripture (and particularly in much of the leadership), we see the outworkings of this in publications like the Sunday school literature I quoted earlier. We also see it in Christian college newspapers such as the following.

Referring to the Bible, one writer states:

> Perhaps it would be better to read it as it was intended to be read, as a variety of texts intended to reveal God's unchanging truth to ancient cultures. Because the Bible was not directly

addressed to our culture, it is important that we read it in its proper context instead of deifying it by reading it literally.[9]

"Deifying it?" Since when does seeing the Bible as relevant across all time and cultures make it an object of worship? Yes, the Bible *was* written in the context of past cultures, and the key to interpreting and understanding Scripture is to consider it in its historical, grammatical, cultural, and literal context. That resulting *interpretation* is the meaning of the biblical text, though it may have varying *applications* from culture to culture and person to person.

One meaning. Many applications.

The Purity of Simplicity

This underscores the fact that the Word of God is for *all* people for *all* time — and it will stand forever. "The grass withers, the flower fades, but the word of our God will stand forever" (Isa. 40:8).

To illustrate this philosophy of using conclusions from outside the Bible to depart from its plain teaching, consider the following. Today, some in the Church claim Paul didn't understand that certain people were supposedly born pre-programmed by their genes to be homosexual.[10] Therefore, they say, Paul's statements condemning homosexual behavior (e.g., in Romans 1) cannot be accepted or meant for today. Paul is accused of a lack of knowledge in this area, so he wrote down "incorrect information" in the Bible. However, remember — the Creator God, who inspired Paul to write the exact words He wanted, has *all* information. With that approach to understanding Scripture (specifically homosexuality), Moses would also be wrong. So would the two angels who visited Sodom and Gomorrah. And so would God Himself, who historically and consistently condemns such a lifestyle.

---

9. "Settling for Second Best: A Search for Truth," *The Crusader*, May 20, 1998, Student Newspaper, Northwest Nazarene College, Nampa, Idaho.

10. Contrary to popular press reports, it has not been established that genes program people to be homosexual. It is true, however, that in this fallen world, we can be predisposed (genetically or otherwise) to certain sins — homosexual behavior may turn out to be one of them. However, as God through Paul said in 1 Corinthians 10:13 (KJV): "There hath no temptation taken you but such as is common to man: but God is faithful, who will not suffer you to be tempted above that ye are able; but will with the temptation also make a way to escape, that ye may be able to bear it."

Even though the customs of people from various cultures in the Bible (e.g., in the Book of Genesis), may well differ from ours, we must treat each custom according to the immediate context of the Scripture passage, *before* attempting to use sources *outside* the Bible to explain it. Because it is God's Word (and not merely a human work), Scripture by definition must be self-authenticating and self-attesting. Therefore, as a first step, Scripture must interpret Scripture. This is not circular reasoning, but rather is supported by Christ's belief in every word of Scripture, and validated to be true by His glorious Resurrection.[11]

Certainly, extra-biblical sources can be used to aid us in understanding the background against which a particular passage was written — but these sources must be secondary to the specific and general context of the words themselves.

Ever since the Fall of man, when Adam chose to "interpret" God's plain words using his own finite understanding, humans have been doubting, and ultimately shaking their fist at Him and His Holy Word.

So it comes as no surprise that those who *do* let God's Word speak plainly to them (particularly in Genesis) are looked down upon with disdain by most of today's scholars, making statements such as,

> Christians are often inclined to take the young-earth position simply because it appears to be the plainest reading of the Bible.[12]

My response is, "Yes! That's right!"

My challenge to the Church and her pastors is simply this: Let us repent of our low view of Scripture, humble ourselves, and learn the lesson God taught the Israelites in Deuteronomy 8:3:

> And he humbled you and let you hunger and fed you with manna, which you did not know, nor did your fathers know, that he might make you know that man does not live by bread alone, but man lives by every word that comes from the mouth of the Lord.

---

11. Matthew 5:18; 1 Corinthians 15:15–22.
12. D. Stoner, *A New Look at an Old Earth* (Eugene, OR: Harvest House Publishers, 1997), p. 37.

Let us also remember Psalm 138:2, "I bow down toward your holy temple and give thanks to your name for your steadfast love and your faithfulness, for you have exalted above all things your name and your *word*" (emphasis added).

If the Church is going to grow, mature, and spread the gospel effectively — if she is ever going to defend the faith and reestablish her presence in the marketplace again, then she *must* return to a high view of the Word of God and a deep reverence for the God of that Word. And this can never happen unless we receive that Word plainly and humbly, as it was meant to be understood. As Christ warned the church at Laodicea, only this kind of repentance will enable us to truly see again (Rev. 3:15–19). This, therefore, is the cure for our blindness and the blandness so prevalent in the Church today.

Chapter 4

Under the Influence

How to Lose a Generation

Something is happening to the 20s generation!

In 2015, Answers in Genesis contracted with America's Research Group (ARG) to conduct research to provide AiG with an idea of America's interest in seeing the life-size ark (under construction in 2015, set to open in 2016). We also sought updated projections from a previous 2008 study.

After considering the results of the 2014 research conducted on those in the Church as is being detailed in this book, we asked ARG to include questions to help us understand what was happening in the culture generationally, specifically with regards to church attendance and people's attitudes towards Christianity. As this was a general population research project (with a 3.8 percent margin of error), we wanted this research to supplement the 2014 research conducted on those who attended church. Specifically, this study investigated the following areas of concern:

- The building of the ark

- The ark location

- Denomination

- Current church attendance

From this 2015 study, we found the following about those in the general population, in regard to church attendance.

Of the 60s age group, 35 percent are disengaged from the Church.[1] The rest attend church regularly or fairly regularly. But of the 20s age group, 64 percent are disengaged from the Church. That is a dramatic generational drop in church attendance! In fact, this is similar to the statistic from the Barna research we quoted in the book *Already Gone* where we state,

> Respected pollster George Barna was one of the first to put numbers to the epidemic. Based on interviews with 22,000 adults and over 2,000 teenagers in 25 separate surveys, Barna unquestionably quantified the seriousness of the situation: *six out of ten 20-somethings who were involved* in a church during their teen years are already gone.[2]

Another statistic from the 2015 research that illustrates the 20s generation has a major problem from a Christian perspective is seen in the answer to the question, "Do you believe people of Christian faith are under attack today?" While 60 percent of the 60s generation answered yes to this question, only 34 percent of the 20s generation answered yes. I do believe (as we will show later on) this reflects the increasing secularization of the 20s generation, and sad reflection on the overall state of the Church.

We also see this decline concerning a Christian worldview in the 2014 research conducted on those who *do* attend church.

Comparing the 40s and 20s generations of churchgoers, (the two groups specifically targeted for this research) we found the following.

When asked, "Is homosexual behavior a sin?" 67 percent of the 40s generation answered yes, but 56 percent of the 20s generation gave the yes answer. When asked, "Should abortions continue to be legal in most instances?" 58 percent of the 40s group said no, but 49 percent of the 20s group gave the no answer. When asked, "Is premarital sex okay?" 34

---

1. This number (64%) includes those in their 20s who attend church once a month or less, only on holidays, and never, and thus are considered disengaged from the church.
2. https://answersingenesis.org/christianity/church/already-gone/.

percent of the 40s generation said yes, but 42 percent of the 20s generation gave the yes answer. Questions about gay marriage and legalizing smoking marijuana revealed similar trends.

Now for the research for the book *Already Gone* (published in 2009), America's Research Group selected those between 20 and 30 who once attended conservative and "evangelical" churches as children. We deliberately skewed the research toward conservatives so that we could all understand that whatever problems showed up would be much worse for the church population in general.

The results? Of these thousand 20 to 29-year-old evangelicals who attended church regularly but no longer do so,

- 95% of them attended church regularly during their elementary and middle school years.

- 55% attended church regularly during high school.

- Of the thousand, only 11% were still going to church during their early college years.

This was one of the most revealing and yet challenging statistics in the entire survey — and something we didn't expect. Most people assume that students are lost in college. We've always been trying to prepare our kids for college (and I still think that's a critical thing to do, of course), but it turns out that only 11 percent of those who have left the Church were still attending during the college years. Almost 90 percent of them were lost in middle school and high school. By the time they got to college, they were already gone! We discovered that about 40 percent are leaving the Church during elementary and middle school years!

This leaves no doubt that there is a downward trend in Christian influence generationally in the culture as a whole, and in the Church.

Brainwashed from Birth

Which leads us to rethink the crucial questions: What does it take to influence a generation? How do you change the way an entire demographic looks at life? How do you alter their sense of what is real and true? If you could fundamentally transform history going forward, how would you go about doing that? How would you ensure that what you drop in humanity's pond will produce concentric rippling effects that continue on for decades. Want to know? I'll tell you.

You target the minds of young people — beginning from when they are born! Many parents have the idea that once their kids are old enough to go to college, they need some instruction to help them cope with whatever attacks may occur on their Christian beliefs. But by then it's way too late. Those attacks start basically when a child is born — and as our research shows, most of those who leave the Church do so because of doubts they succumb to through elementary, middle school, and high school. We should be reminded that many places in Scripture remind parents to be diligent in training their children.

> Train up a child in the way he should go; even when he is old he will not depart from it (Prov. 22:6).

> You shall teach them diligently to your children, and shall talk of them when you sit in your house, and when you walk by the way, and when you lie down, and when you rise. You shall bind them as a sign on your hand, and they shall be as frontlets between your eyes. You shall write them on the doorposts of your house and on your gates (Deut. 6:7–9).

While their minds are still open and impressionable, you create a comprehensive campaign of indoctrination, both covert and overt in nature. And then you repeatedly pound it into them in the most palatable and persuasive ways possible until there is no room left for dissenting views. Unfortunately, this has already happened to most children from the secular world! And if the Church continues sleeping in regard to this tragic trend, then coming generations will become more and more disengaged from the Church — which is exactly what the research is showing.

During the past 30 years of traveling the world and speaking in churches, I have been deeply burdened by distraught parents pleading for advice on how to reach their children who were brought up in the Church but who no longer attend. "How can I reach them?" they ask. "How can we get them back to God and church?"

I've often thought how I'd like to get into the heads of these young adults who have left Church to understand what (and how) they are thinking. What caused them to walk away from the Church (and the truth) they were brought up in?

After teaching thousands of children and adults in churches, I've developed a big picture understanding concerning a number of issues — some of which thrill me (such as the hunger many young people have for answers), while others greatly trouble me.

For example, I've met many young people who no longer see the Church as relevant, nor do they consider the Bible a real book of history that can be trusted. Further, most parents have delegated the spiritual training of their children to the Sunday school, youth group, or some other Christian organization. Additionally, whenever I speak, I typically find that church audiences usually ask the same questions, regardless of what country or church (conservative or liberal) I visit. Among the most frequently asked questions are,

- How can we know the Bible is true and is God's Word?

- Where did God come from?

- Where did Cain get his wife?

- Can't Christians believe in the earth being millions of years old, the big bang, and evolution, as long as they say God was involved?

- Are the "days of creation" regular 24-hour days or millions of years, and does it *really* matter?

- How could Noah fit all the animals on the ark?

- And many more.

As I observed such identical patterns across America, Australia, Europe, and the United Kingdom, I became convinced there must be a connection. I wondered if the lack of teaching biblical apologetics in our churches, youth groups, Sunday schools, and Bible studies could be a major reason why young people leave the Church. As I spoke with parents, I discovered that an overwhelming number of them admitted they didn't know how to answer their children's questions — whether they were about dinosaurs, the age of the earth, or the origin and nature of the Bible. And most churches certainly were not teaching people how to answer such questions. In fact, most church leaders saw such questions as irrelevant, or even taught people that they could believe in evolution, millions of years, etc., as long as they trusted in Jesus (whatever that meant for the people).

The Fruit of Failure

What our research has shown is that the skepticism, doubt, and denial of Scripture's truths so prevalent among college-age students actually begins as young as elementary and *middle school*.

Further, and perhaps more shocking, the research for the *Already Gone* book revealed something many in the Church did not expect — though from my extensive traveling and speaking ministry it did not surprise me. In our survey of 1,000 20-somethings who regularly attended church as children and teens, we asked the question, "Did you often attend Sunday school?" In reply, 61 percent said yes; 39 percent said no! Then our research uncovered something very disturbing. We found Sunday school was actually more likely to be detrimental to the spiritual and moral health of our children.

Of the 20-somethings surveyed, those who went to Sunday school were more likely to be antichurch, defend gay marriage and abortion, and believe in evolution/millions of years than those who didn't go to Sunday school. But we found that the basic cause comes down to being taught the Bible in Sunday school as a book of *stories* (most today regard a "story" to basically mean a fairy tale), rather than real history that can be defended in this scientific age. Also, those who went to Sunday school were more likely to have heard a Christian leader (pastors, Sunday school teacher, etc.) subvert the Bible's authority and accuracy by endorsing evolution/millions of years.

Discussing this in radio interviews, I'm typically asked, "But why the disconnect — after all, surely the churches are teaching the gospel to these children." To which I respond that while that's true, consider where it is we actually get that gospel message. How do we know Jesus rose from the dead? We were not there to see the Resurrection, and we do not have a movie of it, so how do we know it really happened? We know primarily because we trust the authority of the book from which we get the Resurrection account — the Bible. We accept the words of that book as God-breathed, letting them speak to us as coming directly from God.

But these young people we're talking about have been brought up in a culture (and in many cases, churches) where the historical accuracy of Genesis, in particular, has been attacked or greatly undermined. So many have been taught evolutionary ideas and that the world was formed over millions of years. And sadly, most Christian leaders (Sunday school teachers and others) have essentially told these kids that Genesis doesn't matter by telling them they can trust in secularist's version of mankind evolving over millions of years, just as long as they also trust in Jesus. What they do not realize is that this embeds a seed of doubt in these young people's minds — a seed that will take root and later bear much negative fruit. Around 90 percent of churched kids attend a public school where God, the Bible, and prayer have been thrown out. Thus, they are being systematically educated in a secular philosophy of naturalism — which is in reality, atheism.

At school, these children have been effectively taught that the Bible cannot be trusted. Meanwhile, over at the church, these same children are not being taught how to take a stand for the Bible's authority, beginning with the very first verse. They are not trained and equipped to answer skeptical attacks on the Bible. So ultimately, even when the message of Jesus is taught to them, they don't really believe it because their belief in the book from which it comes has already been severely eroded.

Satanic Deception and Human Doubt

Of course, no man or human organization could have the foresight to sit down and plan such a comprehensive strategy of indoctrinating children at school while watering down their faith in Scripture at church. The mere thought of such a strategy smacks of conspiracy theories and paranoid subversive plots. Those who subscribe to ideas like these are often categorized as part of the "lunatic fringe." And yet, believe it or not, according to the Bible, such a strategy *is* being implemented all across the world. Beginning with the first man and woman, Satan planted a seed of doubt and skepticism concerning the character of God and the trustworthiness of His Word. You remember the event. Having been provided with a perfect spouse and a paradise environment, Adam and Eve were in need of nothing. They enjoyed a pristine creation environment and an unimaginable relationship with God. They were fulfilled and satisfied. That is, until the serpent suggested otherwise.

The serpent begins his brainwashing regime by posing a question that, in reality, questions the very word God had just spoken: "Did God actually say, 'You shall not eat of any tree in the garden'?"

Satan launches his strategy by suggesting the possibility Adam and Eve could have misheard, misinterpreted, or misunderstood God's clear command to them. "Are you sure that's what He said? 100 percent positive that's what He meant? Really?" he asked.

From Eve's response, it appears as if the serpent's suggestion has no effect on her, as she recounts almost verbatim what God had commanded them regarding the tree.[3] But here is where Satan's sinks his fangs into Eve's mind. Having successfully slithered up next to her by proposing the possibility of reinterpreting God's truth, he now injects his poisonous venom of lies.

> But the serpent said to the woman, "You will not surely die.
> For God knows that when you eat of it your eyes will be opened,
> and you will be like God, knowing good and evil" (Gen. 3:4–5).

Notice the relationship between the serpent's two statements here. First, he flatly contradicts God's revealed truth, in essence calling God a liar. This was new information to Eve, as she had never distrusted God's Word prior to this. But Satan doesn't stop there. He follows up his claim about God by giving Eve his own apologetic to back up his claim. He convinces her God has knowledge that He is withholding from her and her husband.

Once Eve sees the fruit's beauty and its potential to enhance their lives, she shares with Adam and they eat, and in doing so were bitten themselves. Sin's curse then took root in them. All because they doubted God's Word. And humanity has been doubting and questioning ever since.

It's not news to you that most people today do not see the Bible as having the absolute authority it once did. Pollster George Barna found that in the United States, "A minority of born-again adults (44 percent) and an even smaller proportion of born-again teenagers (9 percent) are

---

3. Concerning God's command regarding the fruit, Eve does add "or touch it." This may be an added prohibition, since in the original command, God only told Adam not to eat from the tree (Gen. 2:17).

certain of the existence of absolute moral truth."[4] Similar surveys in the United Kingdom reveal even lower percentages.

So what has happened? Why the dramatic change? Why is the moral position of previous generations being outlawed more and more? What has driven this moral collapse? Why is this war going on?

Whereas Judeo-Christian thinking once permeated the public education system, today the Christian God, prayer, Bible study, and biblical creation have been virtually erased from the system. Now, generations (including the majority of students from church homes) are being trained in a secular (anti-God) religion. They are being indoctrinated to believe that the universe — and all that exists within it — can be explained (and lived) *without* God by natural processes. And naturalism is just another word for atheism. What these secularists are doing is imposing their religion on the culture. Sadly, many Christians think that when Christian symbols like nativity scenes, crosses, or the Ten Commandments are removed from public places, then it makes the situation neutral. But this is not so. "Whoever is not with me is against me, and whoever does not gather with me scatters" (Matt. 12:30). There is no neutral position.

Sadly, generations today are taught, with increasing intensity, a cosmology, geology, biology, and anthropology that are *all* evolutionary. In essence, these students are being educated *against* the truth of the Bible's history in Genesis, and thus, against its message of salvation and absolute moral standards. This is yet another way Christians and their values are being marginalized in our culture.

But not only are our schools indoctrinating our children this way, but so is the media. Television shows, movies, comic books, video games, advertisements, and so on are all laced with evolutionary thought, subtly (and not so subtly) reinforcing the idea that we are nothing but evolved pond scum, the result of billions of years of natural processes.[5] Molecules in motion and nothing more.

---

4. Barna Research Online, "The Year's Most Intriguing Findings," from Barna Research Studies, December 12, 2000.

5. For example, the more highly evolved "X-Men" and the "millions of years" taught in *Jurassic Park* and *Dinosaurs*. Magazines like *Time, Nature,* and *National Geographic* often feature cover stories touting evolution as fact. And who can ignore the many cable channels, such as Discovery Channel, The History Channel, and Animal Planet, which regularly broadcast shows on animal and human evolution?

Consider that children ages 2 to 17 spend an average of 19.4 hours watching TV each week (Nielsen Media Research, 2000). And this doesn't include the time spent going to movies, playing computer games, surfing the Internet, or reading comic books and magazines. Our children are inundated with messages from the media, which by and large have an evolutionary, anti-Christian foundation.

In the United States, there are approximately 400,000 churches and 6,000 first-run theaters. Which do you think affects our culture more? Unfortunately, the Hollywood writers and producers have more influence on our youth today than our pastors and spiritual leaders.

Sadly, many Christian leaders in the Church have aided the enemy by compromising with evolutionary ideas (either wittingly or unwittingly) through adding millions of years to the Bible, and teaching that evolution and Christianity are somehow compatible. These leaders have, in effect, helped this takeover by reinforcing culture's values and philosophy. The unintended result is that recent generations have begun to reject or reinterpret the Bible's history in Genesis, thus opening a door to undermine biblical authority in general for the other 65 books of the Bible.

But "Theistic Evolutionists" (those who believe in both God and evolution) represent neither theism nor evolution very well, as the two are biblically impossible and mutually exclusive. It should come as no surprise that as generations are trained to disbelieve the Bible's account of origins, the more they doubt the rest of the Bible, as all biblical doctrines (including marriage) are founded (directly or indirectly) in the history found in Genesis 1–11. We see the direct result of this doubt and compromise reflected in the increasing number of moral battles (even in the Church) concerning gay marriage, abortion, and so on. Again, the more people believe evolution and reject Genesis 1–11 as history, the more they will reject the rest of the Bible — including the morality that is based in that history. That's a part of the greater Satanic strategy that had its origin in the Garden.

To practically illustrate this, let's consider some of the results from the ARG research on churchgoers. These are the cumulative results of the 20s and 40s groups surveyed.

When asked, "Did science teachers teach the earth was millions/billions of years old?" 83 percent answered yes. When asked "Did any teachers teach that humans evolved from lower life forms?" 65 percent answered yes. Then when asked, "By the time you graduated high school, did you believe the Bible was less true?" 23 percent said yes! Now think about this with the answer to the question, "Have you ever had anyone teach you how to defend the Christian faith?" and 45 percent said no! Now for those churchgoers who do not believe the Bible is historically accurate, when asked, "What is it that made you begin to doubt the Bible?" 21 percent stated that science showing the earth is old was the reason! There is no doubt the teaching of evolutionary ideas (such as millions of years) has been used to cause many in the coming generations to doubt God's Word — and that doubt easily puts one on a slippery slide of unbelief. And here is a warning for parents and the Church. For the 23 percent who believed the Bible was less true by the time they graduated from high school, 56 percent of them said it was their high school teacher who convinced them the Bible was less true! Not only is this a warning to parents about where they send their children for education, but a warning to Church leaders and parents about the importance of training the coming generations to be able to defend the Christian faith and strengthen their belief in the Word of God.

Conflicting Worldviews

There's an intense battle for the hearts and minds of emerging generations, and churches and homes, by and large, are not preparing people for that battle.

Secularism, with its moral relativism, is in direct opposition to Christianity and its claims of absolute morality. The battle lines are drawn between these two worldviews — one that stands on God's Word and one that accepts man's opinions.

So what will be the outcome of this epic conflict? Can the West return to a Christian worldview that will once again permeate the culture? Yes, it can, but only if there is a return to the authority of the Word of God in churches . . . beginning in Genesis.

Some may wonder why can't we just tell people, "Jesus loves you and has a wonderful plan for your life"? Because as true as that statement is, there are many roadblocks that often prevent non-believers from receiving that love. Scripture tells us that Satan "has blinded the minds of the unbelievers, to keep them from seeing the light of the gospel of the glory of Christ, who is the image of God" (2 Cor. 4:4)

One way this blindness manifests itself is through the pervasive skepticism of our world concerning the Bible. Specifically, people now demand answers concerning how the Bible relates to the real world — like, "Does the Bible deserve credible respect when it speaks about matters of the sciences of biology and astronomy, and also history and anthropology?"

Christians who are fighting for a return to biblical morality cannot hope to win this "war of the worldviews" unless they understand that the real foundational nature of the battle is *biblical authority*, beginning with God's Word in Genesis. This is a primary line of defense that must be upheld without compromise.

The secular world itself already understands this battle — but the Church mostly does not. Therefore, Christian leaders must be awakened by a battle cry. We need to systematically dismantle the false foundation of autonomous human reasoning that leads to an evolutionary mindset by effectively unmasking its folly. And in the Church, we must equip believers concerning how and why God's Word is authoritative and its history of the world foundational to Christian morality and the gospel of Jesus Christ.

So then, practically speaking, what (and who) does Satan's strategy involve? We've already mentioned the role of the classroom and the media, but let's address this a bit more specifically in the context of our enemy's attempt to influence this generation. What does Satan's "Garden Deception" look like today? What questions is he posing to Adam and Eve's descendants? What are some of his modern-day venomous lies?

Defending against Satan's Lies

1. Did God really make you? Is He really the Creator?

We've heard so many times from secular groups like the Freedom from Religion Foundation (FFRF) or the Americans United for Separation of Church and State (AU) that students in science classrooms in public schools can't be taught about creation, as that would be teaching "religion" in government-funded schools. And yet, such secular groups clearly contradict themselves by teaching their own brand of religion (naturalism — atheism) in the public schools. And the government uses our tax dollars to do it.

Imagine for a moment if public school science classes were encouraged to worship the sun. Sound ridiculous? Unfortunately, this is actually happening! But how, and more importantly, how do they get away with it? Well, they just simply call worshiping the sun, "science," and then proceed to teach this "science" in the public schools!

Consider the following quote:

> Our ancestors worshiped the sun. They were far from foolish. It makes good sense to revere the sun and stars because we are their children. The silicon in the rocks, the oxygen in the air, the carbon in our DNA, the iron in our skyscrapers, the silver in our jewelry — were all made in stars, billions of years ago. Our planet, our society, and we ourselves are stardust.[6]

Sounds more like bad science fiction than science, right? And yet, this statement was made by well-known celebrity astrophysicist Neil deGrasse Tyson in the new *Cosmos* series, and teachers are being encouraged to use this series in public school classrooms. Another self-proclaimed evolution expert states the following:

> The Fox television series *Cosmos: A Spacetime Odyssey* hosted by Neil deGrasse Tyson is an excellent way for students at the high school, and even the middle school, level to supplement their learning on various science topics. With episodes that cover almost all of the major disciplines in science, teachers are able to use these shows along with their curriculum to make the topics more accessible and even exciting for learners of all levels.[7]

---

6. Neil deGrasse Tyson in *Cosmos: A SpaceTime Odyssey* (National Geographic Channel, Cosmos Studios, and Fuzzy Door Productions, 2014). Cosmos is a 13-part American science documentary television series that is further marketed for use in classrooms. The show is a follow-up to the 1980 television series *Cosmos: A Personal Voyage*, which was presented by Carl Sagan.

7. Heather Scoville, "Cosmos Episode 4 Viewing Worksheet," About.com, accessed January 26, 2015, http://evolution.about.com/od/Cosmos-Teaching-Tools/fl/Cosmos-Episode-4-Viewing-Worksheet.htm.

Incidentally, Neil deGrasse Tyson is not the first disciple of naturalism in recent times to suggest a distinctly religious message derived from stardust. Tyson's statement echoes one made by prominent atheist Lawrence Krauss (professor at Arizona State University), author of *A Universe from Nothing: Why There Is Something Rather Than Nothing* (2012). In it he casts stardust in the religious role of both "creator" *and* "savior."

Krauss said the following during a lecture:

> You are all stardust. You couldn't be here if stars hadn't exploded, because the elements — the carbon, nitrogen, oxygen, iron, all the things that matter for evolution — weren't created at the beginning of time. They were created in the nuclear furnaces of stars, and the only way they could get into your body is if those stars were kind enough to explode. So, forget Jesus. The stars died so that you could be here today.[8]

So now stars (hydrogen and helium) are "kind" and "sacrificial," while Jesus is obsolete. I get it.

Krauss' own words reveal he is clearly a religious zealot as he proclaims his atheistic, pagan religion. And by doing so blasphemes the true Savior.

Krauss, Tyson, and the producers of the new *Cosmos* series openly draw the battle lines between biblical Christianity and their own substitute religion of evolution. They not only wrongly claim that biblical Christianity is anti-science but also claim that evolutionary science satisfies humanity's spiritual need. Evolution is all you need. But by doing this, they effectively become mouthpieces, pawns of Satan, smugly suggesting, "You don't really still believe God is the Creator, do you?"

Tyson speaks in the series not just about observational science overlaid heavily with his evolutionary claims, but also extols the spiritual satisfaction he derives from his evolutionary beliefs. For instance, in the same episode ("Sisters of the Sun") Tyson says, "Accepting our kinship with all life on earth is not only solid science; it's, in my view, also a soaring spiritual experience." Or in other words, *worship*.

Yet even before the series premiered, the producers made its religious position clear by defining scientific literacy as belief in evolution and

---

8. Lawrence M. Krauss, *A Universe from Nothing*; http://www.goodreads.com/author/quotes/1410.Lawrence_M_Krauss

blaming the exposure of students to creationism for rampant so-called "scientific illiteracy."

On March 11, 2014, AiG writer/researcher Dr. Elizabeth Mitchell wrote this at the beginning of a series of reviews on the new *Cosmos* program she did for the Answers in Genesis website:

> Rebooting the 1980 Carl Sagan series, *Cosmos: A Personal Voyage*, the new 13-part series has a similar goal: to encourage science literacy. Executive producer Seth MacFarlane says, "I think that there is a hunger for science and knowing about science and understanding of science that hasn't really been fed in the past two decades. We've had a resurgence of creationism and 'intelligent design' theory. There's been a real vacuum when it comes to science education. The nice thing about this show is that I think that it does what the original 'Cosmos' did and presents it in such a flashy, entertaining way that, as Carl Sagan put it in 1980, even people who have no interest in science will watch just because it's a spectacle."
>
> MacFarlane blames scientific illiteracy on the "rise of schools questioning evolution" and hopes the series will put an end to the sort of thinking that would question evolution so that scientific literacy can march forward. Ironically, despite the claim that this series is designed to advance science literacy, by adopting Sagan's theme — "The cosmos is all that is, or ever was, or ever will be" — the producers have hoisted a most unscientific flag above this "ship of the imagination."[9]

So it's okay to teach children they really should be worshiping the sun, as Neil deGrasse Tyson states, but it's not okay to teach them the observational science that confirms the account of the history of the universe and earth as given in the Bible.

Which belief is really "imagination"?

Are Christians aware that this activity exists? And if so, why aren't they up in arms about it?

9. Elizabeth Mitchell, "Cosmos Review: 'Standing Up in the Milky Way,'" Answers in Genesis, March 11, 2014, https://answersingenesis.org/reviews/tv/cosmos-review-standing-up-in-the-milky-way/.

Do Christians really understand the anti-God agenda of atheists like Tyson and Krauss? For instance, Professor Krauss also gave a speech in Australia in 2014, proposing how children should be taught about faith in schools, claiming that religious systems shouldn't be treated "as if they're all sacred." He is quoted as stating,

> "Change is always one generation away," the scientist said. "So if we can plant the seeds of doubt in our children, religion [by religion he basically means Christianity] will go away in a generation, or at least largely go away — and that's what I think we have an obligation to do."[10]

That sounds exactly like the method Satan used in Genesis 3 — to create doubt to lead to unbelief. These skeptics are becoming more blatant in aggressively going after the coming generations to indoctrinate them in an atheistic worldview. And sadly, much of the Church and many Christian parents are letting it happen.

2. Isn't Christianity just a "faith-based fairy tale?"

Another way Satan calls into question God and His Word is by questioning the very existence of God Himself. As we've seen, the natural conclusion of evolutionary secularism is that God is no longer considered "necessary." Governments and individuals alike have become *self*-dependent, *exactly* as Satan urged our first parents to become way back in the Garden.

Think of it. If Christianity is not the product of a loving Creator God whose Word is unchanging, infallible, and completely reliable, then what is it?

I'll tell you: *It's simply an illusion. A mind trick. A book of fables, dramatic tales, happy thoughts, and wishes concerning a non-existent afterlife. Nothing more than a man-made story meant to keep bad people in check and make good people feel good about themselves.* This is exactly the conclusion to which atheistic, evolutionary thought and secularism leads. And the more prevalent the belief in evolution becomes, those who embrace it

---

10. http://www.theblaze.com/stories/2014/11/06/prominent-atheist-scientist-cites-slavery-and-gay-marriage-in-this-dire-prediction-religion-will-go-away-in-a-generation/.

become more arrogant and condescending toward God and those who believe in Him and His Word.

By labeling those who believe in biblical creation as "anti-science," they (by direct intention or indirect inference) attempt to discredit Christianity and the Bible from being historically and scientifically accurate and trustworthy. By default, our faith to them is relegated to the same category of those who believe in Greek gods or Santa Claus. To them, God simply *isn't*. Satan would love nothing more than to devalue belief in the existence of God, discredit the person of Christ, and demean His people and His cause in an effort to further his own deceptive, damning agenda.

A "Building Program" Worth Joining

Clearly then, this highlights the urgent need for apologetics. But what kind of apologetics? The biblical issues non-believers question today go beyond traditional presentation of evidence for the Resurrection or the deity of Christ. Therefore, since Satan's strategy is comprehensive, so must ours be, especially as it relates to apologetics. To accurately interpret our culture, we must understand that culture in light of Scripture. Jude wrote that we must "contend for the faith that was once for all delivered to the saints" (Jude 1:3).

Think of what is at stake here. From a human perspective, Christianity as we know it is always just a generation from extinction at any given time. Of course we know from Matthew 16:18 that Christ has pledged to "build His church," ensuring its perpetual existence. But that in no way lessens *our* responsibility in defending and contending for the faith. Like with Timothy, God is counting on us to guard, defend, and share that body of truth we know as the Christian faith (1 Tim. 1:11, 6:20). We have been commanded to "fight the good fight," and we cannot let our Lord down (1 Tim. 1:18, 6:12).

We must help the Church become strong, spiritually and intellectually as we contend for the faith in the marketplace. That is one of the primary missions of the pastor — to "equip the saints for the work of ministry" (Eph. 4:11–12). A healthy and effective church is one that does more than simply dispense messages on "How to Communicate with Your Spouse" or "Steps to Overcoming Stress." We find ourselves in these last days in a wartime scenario. Along with occasional need-based sermons, God's people fundamentally need training on how to confidently engage unbiblical ideas and worldviews. We must be armed with Scripture's truth, God-inspired logic, and the power of the Holy Spirit.

One of AiG's goals is to provide continued training to pastors and Christians through speaking, print, and media resources. But the Church cannot (and was never meant to) shoulder this burden alone. God ordained that the *home* is where this training and equipping begins.

Peter wrote in 1 Peter 3:15, "but in your hearts honor Christ the Lord as holy, always being prepared to make a defense to anyone who asks you for a reason for the hope that is in you; yet do it with gentleness and respect."

Since that is God's command to every believer, shouldn't we begin training toward this at home? I've spoken to scores of parents who feel inadequate to train their children in apologetics. I suspect that one reason for this is that they themselves have never been trained. Many times after I've given a creation apologetics presentation in a church, the pastor will ask where I learned to do this. The pastor then bemoans that he was never taught practical apologetics and really feels ill equipped to answer the skeptical questions of our day that haunt the coming generations. That's why many pastors resort to just teaching spiritual and moral things — but sadly, the coming generations are leaving the Church in droves. However, none of us should feel intimidated by this. All believers can understand and communicate a rational and biblical defense of their faith. There is no good reason why every Christian can't "give an answer" for his/her faith. It is not beyond any of us. But since you cannot share what you don't possess, you must first decide to learn for yourself.

The fact that churched young people are so disconnected from faith and God's Word speaks to the crying need for churches and parents to take on this challenge of equipping the next generation. Still, some may wonder, "Why is all this such a big deal? What's the relationship between destroying a fundamental (and really elemental) belief in a Creator God and the current spiritual/moral state of this generation?"

1. If we are not created by a personal, loving God, then we are, by definition nothing more than random accidents of the universe

(never mind the intellectual suicide required to embrace such an idea/proposition).

2. Without a divine, moral lawgiver, the ultimate (and only) authority for morality and civilization is man himself. On a macro scale, this means we are subject to the changing morality attached to however the winds of culture and government may blow. On a personal level, we are left to our own thoughts and desires, which at best is civil, and at worst is depraved and ungodly.

3. The logical end of such an atheistic philosophy/belief system is existentialism, or the proposition that there is no inherent meaning to life and that nothing actually matters. No afterlife. No judgment or reckoning. And certainly no God before whom you will one day bow.

The natural path of this belief system logically leads us to an undeniable, inevitable conclusion: Do whatever you want to do, because you're nothing more than an evolved animal. You are your own god and self-contained authority. Life is truly meaningless, and when you die you won't know you ever existed. Become an atheist and live an empty life, and then die and never know you were even alive!

This is really the message of much of the public education system today where students are taught as *fact* that life (and the universe) evolved by natural processes (naturalism is atheism). Are we so surprised that kids turn to drugs, sex, suicide, and so on? If evolution is true, why shouldn't they? What difference does it make?

But the message of Christianity is so radically different from the hopelessness atheism promotes. God's Word teaches that man was created with purpose. The life, death, and Resurrection of Jesus Christ has made possible the free gift of eternal life with God for those who receive it, by faith alone, in Christ alone.

Turning the Tables

But Christians don't always have to be on the defensive in these arguments. In fact, it's the *atheist* who should be asked to defend his beliefs and to justify his non-belief in God. With that in mind, try asking the atheist the following questions.

If someone stabs you in the back, treats you like nothing, steals from you, or lies to you, does that ultimately matter in an atheistic worldview where everything and everyone are just chemical reactions doing what chemicals do? Can you really assign blame to them for their actions?

Knowing that you are essentially/ultimately no different from a cockroach in an atheistic worldview (since people are just animals) isn't that disheartening and depressing? That you literally possess no real, intrinsic value.

Doesn't it bother you that atheism (which is based in materialism) has no foundation for logic and reasoning?

Is it tough getting up every day believing that truth, which is immaterial, really has no foundation?

Are you bothered by the fact that atheism cannot account for uniformity in nature (the basis by which we can do real science)?

Why would everything explode from nothing and, by pure chance, form beautiful laws like $E=MC^2$ or $F=MA$?

For professing atheists, these questions can be overwhelming to try to answer within their worldview. Further, within an atheistic framework, atheists are forced to view themselves as God. Instead of saying there *may not* be a God, they say there is *no* God. To make such a statement, they, by default, are claiming to be omniscient (an essential attribute of the God of the Bible). So, by saying there is no God, the atheist refutes his own position by addressing the question as though he or she were God!

Here are more questions for the atheists to defend.

Are you weary of looking for evidence that contradicts the Bible's account of creation and finding none? Do the assumptions and inconsistencies of dating methods weigh on your conscience when they are misrepresented and portrayed as fact?

Where do you suppose all those millions of missing links you base your religion on are hiding?

Doesn't belief in them require more faith (in essence a blind faith) than belief in a God who actually *has* revealed Himself?

If you consider yourself a skeptic, are you ever skeptical of your own skepticism, or of atheism itself?

Don't you feel insecure not being able to explain how everything came from nothing?

Why do you care to live one moment longer in a broken universe where one is merely rearranged pond scum and all you have to look forward to is . . . death, which can be around any corner?

In 467 trillion years, will anyone care one iota about what you did or who you were or how and when you died, because in an atheistic, evolutionary worldview, death is the ultimate "hero"?

Aren't you ready to consider the possibility that you actually aren't "God?" That you could be wrong? Lost? Blind? Mistaken? Ignorant? Sick. Already dead, spiritually? Perhaps in need of answers beyond yourself?

If any self-proclaimed atheist dares to explore that kind of honesty, transparency, and search for truth, then I invite them to reconsider the false religion of atheism. The truth is that atheism is a lie (Rom. 1:25). As a Christian, I understand that truth exists because God exists, who is the Truth (John 14:6). Unlike an atheist, whose worldview doesn't allow him to believe in a foundation for truth or lies, the Bible-believer has a foundation that enables him to speak about that which is true and that which is untrustworthy. This is because those who believe in God have in Him an ultimate authority, the ultimate authority upon which to base such statements.

And here is that truth. There is a God, and you are made in His image (Gen. 1:26, 9:6). This means you (and every other person) have intrinsic value and worth. Whereas consistent atheists teach that you have no value, I see you differently. I see you as a relative (Acts 17:26) and one who — unlike animals, plants, and fallen angels — has the possibility of salvation (a free gift) from eternal death and suffering, which is the result of sin (i.e., disobedience to God; see Rom. 6:23). We have all fallen short of God's holy standard of perfect obedience thanks to our mutual grandfather, Adam (Rom. 5:12). And God sees you differently, too (John 3:16). While you were *still* a sinner, God stepped into history to become a man to die in your place (Rom. 5:8) and offer the free gift of salvation (Rom. 5:15; Eph 2:8–9).

Atheists have no consistent reason to proselytize their faith, but Christians do have a reason — Jesus Christ, who is the Truth, commands us to (Matt. 28:19). We want to see people repent of their evil deeds and be saved from death (Acts 8:22, 17:30). Could there be a greater joy? (Luke 15:10).

Where atheists have no basis for logic and reason (or even for truth, since truth is immaterial), Bible believers can understand that mankind is made in the image of a logical and reasoning God who is the truth. Hence, Christians can make sense of things because in Christ are "hidden all the treasures of wisdom and knowledge" (Col. 2:3). Christians also have a basis to explain why people sometimes don't think logically, due to the Fall of mankind in Genesis 3. The most logical response then is to give up atheism and receive Jesus Christ as Lord and Savior to rescue you from sin and death (Rom. 10:13). Instead of death, God promises believers eternal life (1 John 2:25; John 10:28) and in 467 trillion years, you will *still* have value in contrast to the secular view of nothingness.

The day is coming when we all will give an account before God for our actions and thoughts (Rom. 14:12). Will you repent and receive Christ as your Lord and Savior today so that you will join Christ in the resurrection from the dead (John 11:25; Rom. 6:5)? I challenge you to become an *ex*-atheist, to join the ranks of the forgiven through Jesus Christ, and become a new creation (2 Cor. 5:17).

God is calling Christians at home and in the Church to raise up generations who know what they believe, know why they believe what they do, can defend the Christian faith, can answer skeptical questions, and can preach the salvation message with authority because they believe the authority (the Word of God) from which it comes. Such would change the world!

It's all about influence.

To change a generation, we must begin by training and changing individuals, families, churches, schools and communities. And that begins with *you*.

Chapter 5

The Great Disconnect

Focusing on the Next Generation

We've seen how the Church has already lost much of the 20s generation, and how slow erosion of confidence in both God and His Word typically begins in middle school. We lose them due to the secularized teaching of the public schools, the propaganda through media influence and subtle brainwashing, and through homes and churches that fail to equip and engage their young people in biblical apologetics.

Every generation has the same decision to make: Will I serve the God of the Bible or a false god?

The "god of this world" may shift his seductions slightly from generation to generation, but the basic challenge is always the same. So Christians must be ever vigilant. Every newborn must be taught the truth from scratch or else that soul could be completely lost. While statistics indicate that churches and Christian homes are failing to reach kids, God has given us all the resources we need to turn the tide!

How long does it take to lose a culture, from a Christian perspective?

Actually, it takes only one generation. The devil knows this, and of course God warns us about it. Adolf Hitler understood this when he said, "He alone, who owns the youth, gains the future!"[1]

Over and over again in Scripture, God instructs His people to make sure they train up the next generation.

For instance, when God miraculously enabled Joshua to lead the people through the Jordan River, the first thing He told Joshua to do was to take 12 stones from the riverbed to build a memorial. But what was the memorial for?

Joshua explained, "When your children ask their fathers in time to come, 'What do these stones mean?' then you shall let your children know. . . . the LORD your God dried up the waters of the Jordan for you until you passed over . . . that all the peoples of the earth may know that the hand of the LORD is mighty, that you may fear the LORD your God forever" (Josh. 4:21–24).

The stones were to remind the parents to make sure they taught the next generation about the true God. They were instructed to pass on the knowledge and fear of God to their children.

I think one of the saddest pages in the Bible is in Judges 2:10–12, "And all that generation also were gathered to their fathers. And there arose another generation after them who did not know the LORD or the work that he had done for Israel. And the people of Israel . . . abandoned the LORD, the God of their fathers, who had brought them out of the land of Egypt. They went after other gods, from among the gods of the peoples who were around them."

After Joshua and all the first generation of parents who entered the Promised Land died, the next generation served false gods! It took only one generation to lose the spiritual legacy that should have been passed on.

What happened? In Deuteronomy 6:6–7, God had given clear instructions to the fathers: "These words that I command you today shall be in your heart. You shall teach them diligently to your children, and shall talk of them when you sit in your house, and when you walk by the way, and when you lie down, and when you rise."

---

1. http://www.nizkor.org/hweb/imt/nca/nca-01/nca-01-07-means-46.html.

Obviously, the parents in Joshua's day did not teach their children as they should have — and in one generation, the devil had those kids! While it's ultimately a matter of God's grace that anyone is saved, God has given parents an immense responsibility to do their part. Over and over again, the Jewish fathers were told about their crucial role but they shirked it (see Ps. 78).

Sadly, this same situation already has occurred or is happening now in Western nations once influenced by Christianity. Many fathers today are not carrying out their God-given, God-commanded role to be the spiritual head of their house and to take the responsibility for training their children in spiritual matters.

This generational loss of the spiritual legacy that should be passed on to the coming generations can be seen in ARG's 2014 research on churchgoers. Let's just consider the 20s generation in our churches and what they believe. I trust this is eye-opening and shocking enough to cause parents and Christian leaders to diligently consider how they can address this situation.

Of those in the 20s group who attend church today,

1. 43% do not consider themselves born again

2. 22% believe there are other holy books (other than the Bible) inspired by God

3. Only 21% have read the Bible from cover to cover

4. 22% say the Bible is not true and historically accurate

5. 18% do not believe in the account of Sodom and Gomorrah and Lot's wife becoming a pillar of salt

6. 50% do not believe in a young earth

7. 23% believe God used evolution to change one kind of animal to another kind

8. 19% believe humans evolved from ape-like ancestors

9. 27% believe the Bible has errors

10. 30% believe people don't need to go to church

11. 65% believe if you are a good person you will go to heaven

12. 26% believe the Bible is just a collection of writings

13. Only 45% knew David wrote most of the Psalms

14. 21% didn't know who baptized Jesus

There were many other interesting statistics, but the above is meant to illustrate that there is considerable biblical illiteracy and compromise in the 20s generation in our churches.

Faith, Not Feelings

We live in a culture that teaches us to rely on *subjective experience* rather than *objective truth*. Our studies have shown that "millennials" (those identified as having been born anywhere between the early 1980s to the early 2000s) are not as interested in Christ or Christianity as the previous generation. Further, those who are in the Church have major biblical literacy issues. With the cultural surge of pluralism and an obsession with serving self, even many churches have slid into providing "worshiptainment" for its members instead of equipping them with the Word of God. Thus, there is a whole lot more of entertaining the goats than tending the sheep.

The result is that these millennials in the Church end up with only a thin veneer of biblical understanding (they are familiar with the "stories" in the Bible). However, some appear to be content with this level of knowledge. They cry, "What difference does it make? As long as millennials understand the gospel, who cares if they believe in a literal Adam and Eve or a six-day creation? God's not going to base entrance into heaven based on someone's view of Genesis creation."

True. I would wholeheartedly agree with that statement. Believing in a literal Genesis account is *not* a salvation issue. The Bible is crystal clear that "everyone who calls on the name of the Lord will be saved" (Rom. 10:13), and that "For by grace you have been saved through faith. And this is not your own doing; it is the gift of God, not a result of works, so that no one may boast" (Eph. 2:8–9). Therefore, there is no religious work, good deed, or additional belief attached to saving faith that God requires. It's faith alone. Grace alone. Christ alone.

Period.

However, having settled the issue of salvation, it does not logically follow that nothing else matters from that point on. As critical as they are to Christian doctrine, understanding the complexity of the Trinity or believing in the Second Coming is also not essential in order to be saved — but no respectable believer would deny their fundamental importance to Christian doctrine. Additionally, just because a person is saved doesn't give them the option of now believing whatever they choose about other biblical doctrines and theology which don't speak directly to the issue of salvation. It certainly doesn't give them the freedom to reinterpret a fundamental Christian belief or to suggest an abstract understanding about key passages in Scripture.

Growth Follows Birth

By saying that saving faith in Christ is not ALL that matters, we are saying that there are other important things God would also have us believe and do. Granted, they have nothing to do with salvation, but by definition, Christianity is more than just "becoming a Christian." To say otherwise would be equivalent to saying that being born is all that matters. Food, growth, development, and everything else that follows birth is now optional. What an absurd approach to life!

But this is effectively what some say when they downplay the importance of Scriptures that are fundamental to our understanding of God, His work, creation, the Fall, and the nature of man. It cuts at the very heart of God's ability to accurately reveal and record His own history! And the previously cited research certainly reveals that many in our churches have a problem when it comes to how they view the Word of God.

Of course, all genuine Christians would agree that *obedience to God* is the important thing, that how we live *after* receiving the gospel actually matters.

But let's examine this a bit further. Exactly why is our "Ticket to Heaven" not the only thing we should care about as believers?

First of all, God never says that.

Second, He is clear about many, many other very important truths He wants us to believe and embrace. Otherwise the Bible would contain just one verse about believing in Jesus instead of *66 books* of doctrine and truth!

Third, embedded in true, saving faith is the guarantee of spiritual fruit, particularly the fruit of ongoing faith, obedience, and growth (Matt. 7:15–20, 21–29; Rom. 1:17; Col. 1:20–23; James 2:14–26; Phil. 1:6).

Fourth, it's the *whole* of Scripture that gives us hope, perseverance, and encouragement *after* we come to faith in Christ (Rom. 15:4).

Fifth, ALL of the Bible is inspired and is meant to fuel our faith with nourishment (2 Tim. 3:16–17; 1 Pet. 2:2).

Sixth, God saves individuals so that they might fulfill a greater purpose here on earth. Part of that purpose involves "always being prepared to make a defense to anyone who asks you for a reason for the hope that is in you" (1 Pet. 3:15).

Seventh, there are many important Scriptures that support the truth about Christ and the gospel. To ignore, discount, or demean them is to undercut the foundation of the gospel message itself.

Eighth, you cannot deny one biblical truth without effectually denying many others. For example, you cannot deny the deity of Christ and then believe in Him as Savior. You cannot deny the Resurrection and then still believe in the Cross and its accomplishments. These truths are inseparably linked. Mutually *in*clusive, and bonded with the glue of God's unbroken revelation.

Of course, I know some people say that we should simply avoid controversy and conflict in the world and within certain Christian circles by only focusing on the gospel message itself, and like Paul, "decided to know nothing among you except Jesus Christ and him crucified" (1 Cor. 2:2).

But there are several fatal flaws in this oversimplification of Paul's words. First, no one denies that the gospel message of Christ is what leads sinners to salvation. However, not even Paul limited his evangelistic approach to "Jesus saves," but rather utilized the rest of the Word of God as foundational evidence for his apologetic regarding Jesus. In Acts 17:1–4, Paul reasoned with the Jews using the Old Testament Scriptures. By doing so, he built a solid apologetic case for Jesus being the

Messiah. It was the Apostle's "custom" to reason with both religious leaders and pagans, using the truth of God contained in the Old Testament
Scripture (Acts 17:2). He also took the opportunity when encountering
secular, pagan religious sites to demonstrate to unbelievers that God was
Creator, Judge and Savior (Acts 17:16–34). He even quoted pagan poets
to support his argument (Acts 17:28–29).[2] For Paul, establishing God as
common Creator of all mankind was foundational to his argument and
gospel presentation. Therefore, if God is not Creator, Jesus cannot be
Savior. But you've probably never heard a preacher say that.

All Scripture Matters

This of course is not to say that every time we share the gospel we must
survey the entire redemption story from Genesis to Revelation. It is,
however, to say that the *whole of Scripture* is true and has *direct bearing*
on the truth about Jesus Christ and what He accomplished on the Cross.
Therefore, to focus only on the gospel as our sole beginning *and* ending
point in evangelism is not only without support in Scripture, but also
isn't smart missionary work. And make no mistake about it — we are *all*
missionaries to the pagan culture in which we live.

So in short, yes, it really does matter what you believe *after* you
become a Christian. Theology matters. Sound doctrine matters. All biblical truth — from Genesis 1:1 to Revelation 22:21 is inseparably linked,
connected from truth to truth. You can't merely cut out a particular
portion of Scripture or deny 4,000 years of belief and interpretation
and then replace it with a pagan understanding of that portion of Scripture. We don't have that option with God's Word. Otherwise we become
judges of the Word, exalting ourselves above it. And by doing this, we
are consumed with arrogance, and fall into the same condemnation
incurred by the devil (1 Tim. 3:6).

When reading David's masterpiece of Psalm 119, we encounter 176
stanzas, of which all but 3 expound upon the value, reliability, and personal benefit of God's Word. It's as if David can't stop himself from
highlighting the importance and benefits of Scripture. This becomes

---

2. Here Paul quotes Epimenides, a Cretan poet from 600 B.C. and Aretas, a poet from
Paul's home region of Cicilia (300 B.C.). As Paul spoke without notes, it is impressive
that he had such a recall of secular literature and keen understanding of culture.

even more amazing when you consider that David's "Bible" was basically limited to the first five books of Moses (Genesis through Deuteronomy)!

Being of infinite intelligence, God is totally logical and rational — much more so than man. And throughout Scripture, He clearly indicates when accounts are meant to be understood as illustrations, parables, or metaphors, such as those found in Luke 15:1–32 and John 10:1–7.

Consequently, there is nothing in all of Scripture that gives the slightest hint of the creation or Flood accounts found in Genesis as being anything other than literal, actual, and historical events.

You might be thinking, "I see what you're saying, but practically speaking, what real difference does it make in my daily life whether or not I take those accounts literally? As long as I follow Jesus and obey the truth of His Word, is it really *that* big of a deal?"

That's a good question. So let's answer it by considering the belief in a literal Adam and Eve as an example of how God's "chain of truth" is linked. This exercise will help you connect the dots and see the "domino effect" that truths in Scripture have on one another. Suppose someone claims Adam and Eve were fictional characters created by Moses to illustrate certain truths about God as Creator and mankind as being sinners. Their story, they claim, didn't actually happen as the Bible describes, but rather is more of a parable pointing us to our need for a Savior. So the bottom line is that we see our need for God and come to faith in Christ. How can you say that's a bad thing? As long as the applicable truth is understood, what difference does it make whether Adam was literal or figurative?

To begin with, if God didn't create Adam as a specific individual, then this suggests a massive reinterpretation concerning the origin of man, one that for some Christians lends itself to (theistic) evolution. In that case, at what point in the evolutionary development of man did God impart His image *(imago dei)* into His human creation? Was it when he was still a primate or was there some definitive point over the millions of years evolution requires that God decided one day He was "finished" with man's ascent to full human status? At what point then did sin enter the picture? When, in this evolutionary scenario, did "Adam" become morally responsible for his actions?

Six Days and Salvation

Because Answers in Genesis and other biblical creationists take an authoritative stand on six literal (approximately 24-hour) days of creation and a young (approximately 6,000-year-old) age for the earth and universe, some have mistakenly taken our unwavering stand to mean these beliefs are salvation issues. However, nowhere does the Bible even imply salvation in Christ is conditioned upon one's belief concerning the days of creation or the age of the earth or universe.

For instance, Romans 10:9 states, "If you confess with your mouth that Jesus is Lord and believe in your heart that God raised Him from the dead, you will be saved." It does not state, "If you confess with your mouth the Lord Jesus and believe in your heart that God has raised Him from the dead, and believe in six literal days of creation and a young earth and universe, you will be saved."

Salvation is conditional upon faith in Christ — not belief about the six days of creation or the earth's age. So these are not salvation issues per se. But it is a salvation issue in an indirect sense. Let me explain.

Many Christians, including Christian leaders, believe fossils, the earth, and the universe are millions or billions of years old. I contend that when they accept this timeframe and try to fit millions of years into the Bible, they are violating *three* vital issues.

1. You cannot get the idea of millions of years from the Bible. This idea comes from *outside* of Scripture. When a Christian adds millions of years to the Bible and reinterprets the days of creation or tries to fit this extra time into the first verse in Genesis or a supposed gap between the first and second verses, he is allowing fallible man to be in authority over God's Word. I assert that such compromise (which I believe it really is) is setting an example for others that fallible man can take ideas outside of Scripture and reinterpret God's Word to fit these in.

Ultimately, accepting this view means God's Word is not the final authority and is not without error. It also opens the door to others doing this with other historical claims of Scripture — such as the Resurrection and virgin birth. So it's an authority issue.

But it's also a gospel issue. First, Genesis 1:29–30 teaches that man and animals were originally vegetarian (before Adam's sin). How do we know this for sure? Humans weren't told they could eat meat until after the Flood in Genesis 9:3. This later verse makes it clear that mankind was originally vegetarian, but this changed after the Flood. Verse 30 of Genesis 1 (about animals' diet) is worded in the same way as verse 29 (man's diet), so it makes sense that originally the animals were vegetarian, too.

2. At the end of the creation week, God described everything He had made as "very good" (Gen. 1:31).

3. Genesis 3 makes it clear that the animals (v. 14) and the ground (v. 17) were cursed. And verse 18 makes it clear that thorns came into existence *after* sin and the Curse: ". . . thorns and thistles [the ground] shall bring forth for you."

Now the idea that things have been around for millions of years came from the belief that the fossil record was laid down slowly over millions of years, long before man's existence. So again, when Christians accept millions of years, they must also accept that the fossil layers were laid down before Adam — before the first human sin. Yet the fossil record contains fossil thorns — claimed by evolutionists to be hundreds of millions of years old. How could that be if thorns came after Adam's sin? The fossil record also contains lots of examples of animals that ate other animals — bones in their stomachs, teeth marks on bones, and so on. But according to the Bible, animals were vegetarian before sin.

Also, the fossil record contains examples of diseases, such as brain tumors, cancer, and arthritis. But if these existed before man, then God called such diseases "very good."

Taking all this into consideration, it seems obvious that bloodshed, death of animals and man, disease, suffering, and thorns came *after* sin. So the fossil record had to be laid down after sin as well. Noah's Flood would easily account for most fossils.

But what does this have to do with a gospel issue? The Bible calls death an "enemy" (1 Cor. 15:26). When God clothed Adam and Eve with coats of skins (Gen. 3:21), a good case can be made that this was the first death — the death and bloodshed of an animal. Elsewhere in Scripture we learn that without the shedding of blood there is no remission of sins (Heb. 9:22), and the life of the flesh is in the blood (Lev.

17:11). Because Adam sinned, a payment for sin was needed. Because sin's penalty was death, then death and bloodshed were needed to atone for sin. So Genesis 3:21 would describe the first blood sacrifice as a penalty for sin — looking forward to the one who would die "once for all" (Heb. 10:10–14).

The Israelites sacrificed animals over and over again, as a ceremonial covering for sin. But Hebrews 10:4 tells us that the blood of bulls and goats can't take away our sin — we are not physically related to animals or ascended from them. We needed a perfect human sacrifice. So all this animal sacrifice was looking forward to the one called the Messiah (Jesus Christ).

Now if there was death and bloodshed of animals before sin, then this undermines the atonement. Also, if there were death, disease, bloodshed, and suffering before sin, then such would be God's fault — not our fault! Why would God require death as a sacrifice for sin if He were the one responsible for death and bloodshed, having created the world with these bad things in place?

One of today's most-asked questions is how Christians can believe in a loving God with so much death and suffering in the world. In fact, in the 2014 ARG research on the Church, nearly 20 percent of the 20s generation said their faith had been challenged by someone asking why bad things happen. The correct answer is that God's just Curse because of Adam's sin resulted in this death and suffering. We are to blame. God is not an unloving or incompetent Creator of a "very bad" world. He had a loving plan from eternity to rescue people from sin and its consequence of eternal separation from God in hell.

So to believe in millions of years is a gospel issue. This belief ultimately impugns the character of the Creator and Savior and undermines the foundation of the soul-saving gospel. It's an authority issue — is God's Word the ultimate authority on all matters of life and practice?

So, if evolution were true, then this evidence of sin (disease and death) entering the world occurred *before* the first homo sapien (man) appeared. This notion is a clear contradiction of the entire biblical narrative regarding creation, mankind, and sin. In reality, man (Adam) first sinned, *then* disease and death appeared, not before. Therefore, to claim to be a Christian and believe in evolution is to, in the strictest sense of the word, be *ignorant* of the Bible as well as the logical and theological flow of truth recorded in it.

A Real Adam and a Real Jesus

Another problem with interpreting Adam as figurative is that all those who subsequently understood Moses' written account of Adam as a literal, created man would then be mistaken, including: the Jewish people, the author of Chronicles (1:1), Job (31:33), Dr. Luke, who traces Jesus human genealogy back to Adam (Luke 3:38), Jesus Himself[3] (Matt. 19:4) Paul (Rom. 5:14; 1 Cor. 15:22, 45; 1 Tim. 2:13–14) and Jude (1:14). All these held a literal interpretation of the first man, Adam. In fact, Paul goes so far as to make a direct parallel between Jesus' historicity, deeds, and impact on humanity with Adam's. In Romans, he writes,

> Therefore, just as sin came into the world through *one man*, and death through sin, and so death spread to all men because all sinned — for sin indeed was in the world before the law was given, but sin is not counted where there is no law. Yet death reigned from *Adam* to Moses, even over those whose sinning was not like the transgression of *Adam, who was a type of the one who was to come.*
>
> But the free gift is not like the trespass. For if many died through one man's trespass, much more have the grace of God and the free gift by the grace of that one man Jesus Christ abounded for many. And the free gift is not like the result of that one man's sin. For the judgment following one trespass brought condemnation, but the free gift following many trespasses brought justification. For if, because of one man's trespass, death reigned through that one man, much more will those who receive the abundance of grace and the free gift of righteousness reign in life through the one man Jesus Christ.
>
> Therefore, as one trespass led to condemnation for all men, so one act of righteousness leads to justification and life for all men. For as by the one man's disobedience the many were made

---

3. But we must also understand that because Jesus is the Word, then every Word in Scripture is the Word of Jesus.

sinners, so by the one man's obedience the many will be made righteous. Now the law came in to increase the trespass, but where sin increased, grace abounded all the more, so that, as sin reigned in death, grace also might reign through righteousness leading to eternal life through Jesus Christ our Lord (Rom. 5:12–21, emphasis added).

Here Paul compares and contrasts Jesus' historicity and gift of salvation to mankind to the historicity and sin of Adam. It's a direct, intentional, one-to-one association. In an effort to argue for the gospel's essence and power, Paul links the factual reality of Adam's existence and deeds compared to those of Jesus. If the one (Adam) didn't actually do what he did (sin), then the other (Jesus) didn't do what He did (bring salvation). He does this again in 1 Corinthians 15:45. You cannot have a savior without an original sinner. Take away God's example of original sin and His argument for the efficacy of Jesus' sacrificial death is made void.

Moses was pretty confident when it came to the facts about Adam. He knew so much about this man Adam that he even tells us how old he was when he died! (Gen. 5:5). If evolution were true and the Genesis account were symbolism or allegory, it would have also taken God millions of years to create Eve from Adam's rib!

The bottom line is that all of Scripture is in agreement that Adam was a literal, historical man, formed in a single act of creation, not the result of millions of transitionary, human-like species. So can you see how removing just one literal truth from a few thousand years ago affects the rest of the Bible, theology, and eternal salvation?

So if the Bible cannot be trusted historically, then it is flawed and cannot be trusted in areas of greater significance, such as heaven, hell, marriage, sexual identity, family, etc. If Moses got it wrong (along with Jesus, Paul, and others), then how can we say, "*All* Scripture is inspired?" More importantly, how can we say Jesus is God if He didn't even know the difference between history and mere *story*? But in fact, He *does* know the difference, as He consistently used illustrations and parables to teach the multitudes. But at no time did He ever come close to mistaking one for the other. He also accepted the Old Testament as a literal and reliable account.

By contrast, the interpretative methods used in Genesis by many Christians who believe in millions of years are not interpretative decisions that most biblical scholars would apply to any other place in Scripture! So why do they pick on Genesis? Well, because these Christians tell us that "science" (practiced by fallible scientists) has shown us that we need to believe in millions of years, and thus we must fit these long ages into the Bible — even though they do not fit!

A religion professor once accused me (and by association all Christians who take God at His Word) of weaving a "web of lies" concerning the Genesis account. Of course, the saddest part of that accusation is that he ultimately is calling God a liar. But the Scripture itself states, "God is not man, that he should lie" (Num. 23:19).

100% True from the Beginning

Genesis is clear. The account of biblical creation we hold to comes straight out of God's Word, so to claim that it's a lie is to accuse God of being a liar. And if God lied in Genesis, then where did He stop lying? And what does that say about our Holy God's character?

I remember a young lady once telling me that her pastor was preaching from Genesis and telling the congregation that what was stated was just a myth used to explain religious truth. This pastor insisted people had to believe evolution and millions of years and thus couldn't take the account in Genesis literally. This lady was a young Christian, so she went to the pastor and asked, "So when does God start telling the truth in His Word?"

Good question — and God's Word has the answer:

> Thy word is true from the *beginning* (Ps. 119:160; KJV, emphasis added).

Some have claimed that biblical creation is simply my "own dubious understanding of Christianity," but it just so happens that biblical creation has been by far the dominant view of creation for most of Christian history as well as for the Jews *before* Christ. It is those compromising positions like theistic evolution, the gap theory, the day-age theory, the framework hypothesis, or progressive creation (or the many others that pervade the modern Church) that are newcomers to the scene. Those views developed only after geologists abandoned Scripture and began assigning old dates to the rock layers! The reason most scholars and people of the past two hundred years believe those compromising positions has nothing to do with what the Bible says in Genesis. Rather, it's because they've been influenced by secular beliefs about man's past — particularly the belief in millions of years. Beliefs that were birthed and nourished due to a calculated rejection of God's Word!

Now, it is true that some people who have been taught to trust the Bible from the very first verse still abandon Christianity. Satan continues to be very clever at drawing people away from God. Remember, having faith is not simply a matter of being exposed to enough evidence. Even some of those who saw Jesus raise the dead didn't believe (Luke 16:31)! People walk away from the faith for many different reasons, and they are not always intellectual ones. That being said, studies we've done in partnership with America's Research Group show that the vast majority of young people are walking away from the faith because they *doubt God's Word*. So while having good, solid answers does not always guarantee faith, it certainly does help, and we receive hundreds of testimonies from people who have been strengthened in their faith or brought back to the faith because of our ministry.

This is why we published the book *Already Gone* in 2009. If you haven't read this, I encourage you to do so and find out what real scientific research has found in regard to young people leaving the Church.

Others, in an attempt to discredit the belief in biblical creation, have referred to it as an "idol." But idolatry is placing something or someone above God Himself. Simply believing what God's Word says and defending it can hardly be considered idolatry. On the contrary, it is honoring God even more when you take Him at His Word and respect it. And those who do so are only upholding and proclaiming God's Word as Christians have done for centuries. The Word of God is "living and powerful" and certainly an impenetrable rampart because it is "flawless" (Prov. 30:5; NIV) "truth" (John 17:17) that "endures forever" (Isa. 40:8) and will "never pass away" (Luke 21:33).

So can you see how God's Word is bound together by its own character? To contain an error, particularly one that relates to creation, sin, Christ, and salvation would cast a dark shadow of doubt over the entire Bible, and rightfully so. When Paul says "all Scripture" (Greek: *pasa graphe* or "every individual portion of Scripture") is "inspired by God" (2 Tim. 3:16; NLT), he means exactly what he says. Jesus affirmed this belief in the totality of God's written revelation when He said (referring to the "Law and the Prophets," i.e., Moses' first five books and the rest of the Old Testament),

> For truly, I say to you, until heaven and earth pass away, not an *iota*, not a *dot*, will pass from the Law until all is accomplished" (Matt. 5:18, emphasis added).

Christ was so specific that He goes beyond merely affirming the accuracy of the Bible's general themes, historical accounts, or its individual truths. No, He goes even further by saying that God's commitment to the integrity and reliability of His Word goes all the way down to the very letters (iota) and punctuation (dot) of Scripture!

Therefore, all of God's truth in Scripture fits and works together, seamlessly and without flaw. What we are facing today, however, is a generation that cannot link theological "cause and effect" together. Instead, they approach God's Word "buffet style," picking and choosing what truths and beliefs are most attractive to them, while rejecting those truths that are less likely to be mocked in the marketplace. And this will continue as long as they remain untrained and unequipped in biblical truth and apologetics.

A low view of Scripture also has a "domino effect," leading not only to biblical illiteracy, but also to theological bankruptcy, doctrinal error, and spiritual anemia. This trend in the Church must be reversed. And it *can* be. But in order to do so, we must help this generation begin taking ownership of their faith (more about that in the next chapter).

As a final section for this chapter, and to ensure that people do not misunderstand what is being said, let me specifically deal with our stand on a young earth in relation to the topic of biblical authority.

Many Christians believe in millions of years and are truly born again. Their belief in millions of years doesn't affect their salvation. But what does it do? It affects how other people, such as their children or others they teach, view Scripture. Their example can be a stumbling block to others. For instance, telling young people they can reinterpret Genesis to fit in millions of years sets a deadly example: they can start outside Scripture and add ideas into Scripture.

Ultimately, this approach eventually suggests that the Bible is not God's infallible Word. This creates doubt concerning God's Word — and doubt often leads to unbelief. Eventually, they may reject Scripture altogether. And since the gospel comes from a book they don't trust or believe is true, there's nothing to prevent them from rejecting the gospel itself.

So the age of the earth and universe is not a salvation issue per se — somebody can be saved even without believing what the Bible says on this issue. But it is a salvation issue indirectly in that all Scripture is inseparably linked, particularly regarding core doctrine. Pull out one of these foundational stones and the entire structure of Scripture is affected.

Today, there is a crying need to teach the coming generations to stand uncompromisingly, boldly, and unashamedly on the whole Word of God, beginning in Genesis.

Chapter 6

Owning Up — Embracing a Faith of Your Own

The Ultimate Handoff

In any relay race, the passing of the baton is critical. The transfer of that nearly weightless hollow metal tube determines who goes home with gold, and who simply *goes home*. Runners do not show up the day of the race and simply "wing it." Instead, there are countless hours spent on the track practicing their exchange, with the eventual race itself becoming the result of hundreds of similar previous transfers.

If the one possessing the baton performs his/her job effectively, the baton is passed and the race goes on. Of course, the one receiving the baton also has a responsibility. Unless he is open to accepting it, and grips it firmly, the baton may be dropped and the race lost.

I believe the Christian faith is very much like a relay race. One generation carries the responsibility to pass on the faith to the next. When that generation dies, the generation that remains becomes responsible to carry on the gospel to their world, and to faithfully place it in the hands and hearts of their physical and spiritual children. Since A.D. 33, the baton

of faith has been passed — and sometimes dropped. And to the degree
that those who pass on the faith and those who receive it do their job,
Christianity will continue. But as we have seen from the new research
ARG conducted, the Church is currently failing at this critical task in
many areas in the West.

In England, two-thirds of young people now say they don't believe
in God — in a culture where most people once went to church.

In America, about two-thirds of young people will leave the Church
once they live on their own. As I have stated before, Answers in Genesis
commissioned America's Research Group to find out why this is happening and published the results in the book *Already Gone* in 2009. It
revealed that these kids began doubting and disbelieving the Bible at a
very young age.

We also established that around 90 percent of those who leave
Church attended public schools, where, by and large, God, creation, the
Bible, and prayer (in other words, Christianity) were thrown out long ago.
Atheistic evolution, however, is taught as fact. The vast majority of these
students represented in our research were not taught apologetics (how to
give a reasoned defense of the Christian faith) in their homes or churches,
so they don't believe it themselves and certainly can't defend it to others.

The public schools have been teaching their own brand of apologetics: how to defend the idea of evolution and history over millions of
years, thus causing multitudes of U.S. students from Christian homes to
doubt the history in Genesis. Doubts about Genesis place young people
on a slippery slide of unbelief that eventually destroys their confidence
in the rest of Scripture. Their trust in the soul-saving gospel itself, which
is grounded on the Bible's historical claims, is also undermined.

Even when parents pull their kids out of public school, the anti-God
message is so prevalent in the media, museums, and colleges — and
even among friends, neighbors, and workmates — that young people are
woefully unprepared to understand and defend their beliefs. Let's face it.
We live in a pagan, post-Christian society, not a Christian nation. We
should therefore not be surprised when most people and institutions are
godless, anti-Christian, and anti-Bible. But tragically, even many leaders in Christian education have compromised with evolution and earth

history over millions of years. Many groups are now even producing homeschool curricula that promote evolution and millions of years!

The Secularization of America

Joseph Stalin certainly knew the power of education as a propaganda tool. In just one generation, he converted hordes of the deeply religious Russian people into followers of atheistic Marxism. He said, "Education is a weapon, the effect of which is determined by the hands which wield it."[1]

Sadly, most of the people who control the West's publishing and video industries today reject the God of the Bible, and they are winning over the next generation, indoctrinating them in evolutionary humanism. Day after day, our children are bombarded with their message.

The consequences in America were again confirmed in October 2012, when the Pew Forum on Religion and Public Life released new survey results. The CNN website reported, "The fastest growing 'religious' group in America is made up of people with no religion at all, according to a Pew survey showing that one in five Americans is not affiliated with any religion. . . . The survey found that the ranks of the unaffiliated are growing even faster among younger Americans. Thirty-three million Americans now have no religious affiliation, with 13 million in that group identifying as either atheist or agnostic, according to the new survey."[2]

For years, I have been warning churchgoers about this danger in my presentations. Despite the fact America has many megachurches and more Christian resources than any other country in history, as a culture we are becoming more secular every day. America is heading down the same path as Europe and England.

The CNN item reported that atheist and secular leaders were elated by the Pew poll. Jesse Galef, communications director for the Secular Student Alliance, expected the growth to translate into greater political

---

1. Amy R. Caldwell, John Beeler, Charles Clark, *Sources of Western Society Since 1300,* "Joseph Stalin: An Interview with H.G. Wells" (Boston, MA: Bedford/St. Martin's, 2011), p. 516.
2. Dan Merica, CNN, "Survey: One in Five Americans Has No Religion," October 9, 2012, http://religion.blogs.cnn.com/2012/10/09/survey-one-in-five-americans-is-religiously-unaffiliated/.

power for secular interests: "As more of the voters are unaffiliated and identifying as atheist and agnostics, I think the politicians will follow that for votes. We won't be dismissed or ignored anymore."[3]

Just before the poll was released, Bill Nye the "Science Guy" (from a popular 1990s TV program) expressed the agenda of today's elite in public education and the media. In a video entitled *Creationism Is Not Appropriate for Children*, Nye basically says if children aren't taught evolution as fact, America will lose its edge in science, and no longer have engineers and other innovators. Bill Nye, incidentally, was voted humanist of the year in 2010. His words reflect the growing, deliberate agenda of the media elite to capture the next generation for the secular humanists.

In an article by a staffer from the National Center for Science Education (an organization begun in 1983 for the explicit purpose of attacking the influence of biblical creationism and now headed by ardent evolutionist Brian Alters), it is very clear that the atheists today are out to indoctrinate our kids.

The last paragraph of the article reads, "What we can do is work toward the day when American school children are taught evolution in the same way as any other well-established scientific idea, without caveats or apologies. With evolution at the center of biology, and thus important to the success of medicine, biotechnology, and agriculture, we can't afford to keep it bottled up or to kick the can."[4]

Plainly stated, atheists don't want Christians teaching kids about God — they want to teach your kids there is no God! They really are out to get your kids, and they are using the public schools, secular media, museums, and other outlets to do this. The public schools (despite a minority of Christian teachers who are trying to be missionaries in the system) have mostly become churches of secular humanism.

Yes, the atheists, like Hitler and Stalin, know that if they can capture the next generation (through the education system, media, etc.), they will have the culture.

---

3. Ibid.
4. Steven Newton, "Creationism, Mr. Nye, and Dr. Pepper," Huffington Post Blog, http://www.huffingtonpost.com/steven-newton/creationism-mr-nye-and-dr-pepper_b_1934407.html.

Beyond Bible Facts

Christians need to take heed of God's Word and ensure they are capturing the next generation for the Lord — passing that spiritual legacy along to the children, so they will not be captured by the world!

Yes, it takes only one generation to lose a culture, and America is on the brink of such a change right now! God's people need to wake up and understand a battle for their kids is raging around them — a battle that is being won, at the present time, by those who seek to destroy the next generation spiritually.

In view of such relentless indoctrination that bombards our young people every day, giving a couple of 30-minute lessons at church or home isn't enough. While many parents have already opted to put their kids in Christian schools, weekly church programs, and homeschools, few appear to be doing a very good job filling in the gaps. More is needed.

Teaching young people how God's Word — rather than the atheistic worldview — makes sense of our world requires intense study, commitment, and fervent prayer. The Church and parents must reevaluate their old assumptions about the way we should be teaching our kids in a hostile culture, and work together to build the next generation by following the directives from God's Word.

Our research published in 2009 demonstrated that the majority of our churched kids drop out of church by college age. Sadly, many never return — although the research also showed great potential for many to do so.[5] And though we've already shown several reasons for this falling away, one stands out pretty clear. So why do they lose the grip on the baton?

One of the key reasons why kids don't embrace their parent's/church's faith in adulthood is because they never learned how to "own" their own faith. They never asked tough questions about their faith in a safe environment. Perhaps they were raised in a church or home where questions and doubts were discouraged. Whatever the case, they never worked through some of these difficult issues while they were young; therefore never being challenged with *what* they believe or *why* they believe it.

---

5. Ken Ham and Britt Beemer, *Already Gone* (Green Forest, AR: Master Books, 2009).

The ARG research on the 20s and 40s groups that class themselves as churchgoers, showed that when asked, "Has anyone ever challenged you and your Christian faith?" only 23 percent said yes. When those who were challenged were asked, "At what time in your life were you challenged?" the answers were middle school 13 percent, high school 24 percent, college 24 percent, after college 40 percent.

When a believer's faith is challenged by the world, friends, the classroom, or even self-doubt, we must pause to address those answers from Scripture. This is how ownership of one's faith is made strong. Before we can give an answer to others concerning our faith, we must first develop a *personal apologetic*. After being born again and growing spiritually, the next season of your spiritual life is to embrace personal responsibility for your own faith. Doing this births confidence and breeds courage in the heart of those who follow Jesus Christ in a world filled with skeptics and scoffers.

Here are some questions to ask regarding the next generation in our homes and churches:

- Do they really know what they believe? Do they understand the basic doctrines of the Christian faith?

- How do we prevent them from simply "parroting" back what they've heard others say, like parents or youth leaders?

- How can we create an environment of honesty and transparency so that they don't merely accept God's truth as a way to please (or appease) parents and other adults?

- What are the questions they are going to be confronted with so we can make sure they are equipped with answers?

For instance, the ARG research on churchgoers dealt with what those who were challenged about their Christian faith had to say. Without giving any suggestions, the people surveyed provided the topics that were brought up. Here are the results in order beginning with the biggest: 24 percent age of the earth; 18 percent why only Christians go to heaven; 16 percent why bad things happen to people; 15 percent how one can believe the Bible.

Sadly, many church leaders (see the research from the book *Already Compromised*[6]) will tell Christians they can believe in millions of years — and yet this is one of the main issues used to challenge people's Christian faith. And, as discussed in the previous chapter, this is an issue that undermines Bible authority and the gospel.

We would all agree that our kids have a crucial need to take ownership of their faith, for unless they do, they will likely cast off their Christian beliefs like an old sweater as soon as they are no longer relevant or perceived as necessary, or when they can't answer questions that undermine the Christian message. Like a rocket booster that has burned out its fuel, our kid's Christianity may also burn out as soon as they hit the city limits. They may put on a Christian facade when they're home, but in reality their faith is practically useless.

The Journey from Doubt to Confidence

Picture in your mind a bridge. This metaphorical bridge represents the passageway from ignorance and doubt to confidence and taking ownership of your faith. It pictures your journey of embracing and maturing in a personal faith in God. This bridge spans a deep chasm, a huge abyss, below which are the jagged rocks and roaring rapids of spiritual disaster. Many young Christians never make it all the way across this bridge. Some tumble over the side when the strong winds of doubt and hard times blow against them. Their beliefs fall with them and are crushed to bits on the rocks below. Others grow afraid as they cross this bridge, becoming paralyzed at the prospect of going forward by faith. They freeze as they look down, dwelling on their doubts. Meanwhile, others pass them by. Still more turn back for fear they will stand alone in the world upon their arrival on the other side. The time comes in every Christian's journey of faith when he/she must journey across this "bridge."

Crossing this bridge means gaining a firm grasp of Scripture. It means understanding how the Bible's truths are tightly woven together, inseparably linked with one another. Walking across this bridge means embracing Jesus Christ and what He has done for you. It means learning to process and apply the truths of Scripture to everyday life and to be

6. Ken Ham and Greg Hall, *Already Compromised* (Green Forest, AR: Master Books, 2011).

able to "give an answer" that you can "contend for the faith that was once for all delivered to the saints" (Jude 1:3). It signifies that you stand for all that Christ stands for. It means forming a personal apologetic based on Scripture.

The word *apologetic* comes from the Greek word *apologia*. It is usually translated "answer" or "defense" in 1 Peter 3:15: "But sanctify Christ as Lord in your hearts, always being ready to make a defense to everyone who asks you to give an account for the hope that is in you, yet with gentleness and reverence" (NASB).

If Christianity is true, and the Bible is the infallible, inspired Word of God, Christians should be able to defend their faith when asked skeptical questions. This doesn't mean that we automatically know all the answers — but from a big-picture perspective, we should be able to give a reasoned argument to counter attacks on the Christian faith. Unfortunately, most Christians have not been taught practical, basic apologetics (and from our research, they don't even recognize they haven't been taught). Consequently, they don't know how to adequately defend the Christian faith when it is challenged. This new research on churchgoers illustrates that many in our churches really have problems with the very basics of Christianity. For example, our research yielded the following results:

- 39% said they attend church but are not born again.

- 95% say that all the books of the bible are inspired, but 22% believe there are other holy books inspired by God — and 21% say the Bible is not true and historically accurate! So what do many of these people mean when they say the Bible is "inspired." I suggest many have never been taught what "inspired" means, therefore they don't understand it.

Now here is a very telling statistic:

- 45% say no one ever taught them to defend the Christian faith! No wonder we have problems with the coming generations! In the book *Already Gone* we emphasized, based on research (and on what happened to those who attended Sunday school) that most churches and Christian homes are not teaching apologetics.

Now, crossing the bridge of ownership I mentioned earlier also requires much time, and though you reach certain milestones of growth and understanding along the way, it actually involves a *lifetime* of discovery, dedication, and faith. There is no time or room to stand still on this bridge. Every believer must decide whether or not he or she will move on toward the other side. Behind you, back on the mountainside, are those who are merely "renting" someone else's faith and beliefs (their parent's, youth leader's, pastor's). They are either too afraid or too preoccupied with other things to take a step of faith onto this bridge. From where they stand, they're still not sure this bridge will hold their full weight. These people will never move forward in their faith. Their fear, unbelief, and unwillingness to walk with God disqualifies them from truly possessing a faith of their own.

But others have crossed this bridge before. They have proven its worth, strength, and reliability. Ahead, on the other side, are those who have owned their own faith. They have assumed the responsibility of examining the Scripture and interacting with their God. They have tested the faith and tasted the goodness of the Lord, and He has not let them down (Ps. 34:8; Rom. 1:16–17, 10:11). Since the book *Already Gone* was published, I have heard numerous testimonies of how parents and churches had begun teaching apologetics to equip people to defend the Christian faith. Thousands of churches decided to use the Answers in Genesis evangelistic Bible Curriculum (Answers Bible Curriculum: A for Apologetics; B for Biblical authority; C for Chronological), and the Answers in Genesis VBS programs (that have an emphasis on biblical authority and apologetics and are very evangelistic). The feedback has been exciting — so many saying this has revolutionized the younger generations and even made the older generations realize what has been missing from much of the Church in recent times.

So which way are you heading today? Which way are your children headed? What about the young people in your church?

A Faith That Doesn't Fizzle

Every Christian receives his or her faith from someone else. As we've seen, like a baton in a relay race, faith is handed over from one person to another. It's the passing on of a spiritual legacy. Thinking back over your life, who has helped pass the faith on to you? What attitudes/perspectives did you learn or catch from them? I praise the Lord for Christian parents who passed a wonderful spiritual legacy on to me. They taught me not only to stand boldly and unashamedly on God's Word, but also how to answer skeptical questions and to never knowingly compromise God's Word! How I pray that this would be so for every parent as they train their children. As I've said so many times, the ministries of Answers in Genesis, the Creation Museum, and the Ark Encounter involve a legacy of parents who passed on a spiritual legacy to their children.

So how do we do our best to pass on a faith that won't fizzle over time? First, we must give them *reasons* to believe. That's the meaning implicit in Peter's admonition to "give an answer" and is the very essence of apologetics. Having reasons behind their beliefs puts "steel" in their faith. And perhaps at no other time in history has such strength been needed. In an age of pluralism, atheism, and skepticism, a "Sunday school" faith built on stories alone won't cut it out there in the real world. Instead, our children's faith will be easily and quickly devoured by worldly philosophy, demonic deception, and unbelief. And from the ARG research, it's very obvious there needs to be teaching in apologetics in two main areas:

1. General Bible apologetics (how do we know the Bible is true; what does it mean that it's inspired; how do we know Jesus is God, etc.)

2. Creation apologetics (one of the challenges most often posed to Christians is the attack on biblical authority, beginning in Genesis, e.g., how did Noah fit the animals on the ark; doesn't carbon dating disprove the Bible; where did Cain get his wife; how could all the people today come from Adam and Eve; what about evolution, dinosaurs, the age of the earth, the big bang, etc.)

So what's involved in taking ownership? Here are some practical suggestions on how to foster personal ownership of faith for the next generation:

- Help them discover the foundations of their faith and why they believe, not only through teaching, but also through personal interaction and small group discussion.

- Never avoid the hard questions. God is not threatened by our confusion or questions. He can handle them. And His Word can give us direction and insight when faced with mystery and apparent contradictions in Scripture.

- Never judge a young person for asking what may be considered a "taboo" question in some Christian circles, such as, "How do we know the Bible is really God's Word?" or "Why is Jesus so different from the angry God of the Old Testament?" or "If God is so real, why don't more people believe in Him?" or "Why are we the only ones who believe in a literal account of Genesis? Why does it seem like its 'us against the world'?"

  It is critical that young people feel free to voice their thoughts, doubts, and struggles without fear of ridicule or condemnation. Unless this generation is allowed to do this, they will likely either become hardened and bitter, walk away from the faith, or politely suppress negative feelings and thoughts about God in order to appear compliant and obedient.

- Let *them* come up with the reasons why God, the Bible, and the Christian life seem so hard to understand at times. Young people are in touch with where their generation is. They aren't concerned with reaching adults, but are living in the "now" with their own age group. By addressing the questions their generation is asking, we help them face contemporary apologetic difficulties head on.

- Challenge their answers. Ask "Why?" and "What do you mean by that?" Force them to think through what they're saying/ believing as well as why.

- Don't be afraid to create a little tension. Play the role of "devil's advocate." Don't provide all the answers. Don't hesitate to end your discussions with unanswered questions.

- Pick the top ten issues your kids are facing in their world and use them as a way to help them understand what they believe (evolution, sex, abortion, moral relativism, sexual identity, etc.).

- It's our job to create an environment where hard questions and doubting are encouraged.

- Praise them for their honesty, insights, and thoughtful questions.

- Give them individual assignments in which to study and research on their own regarding some of the hard questions you discuss.

- Provide resources (books, articles, websites, videos) for them to use. This is why we do what we do at AiG. We are here to serve you! We are a resourcing ministry raised up to help provide answers to the challenging questions of our day.

As I mentioned before, many churched young people today are simply carrying around someone else's faith — their parent's, or their church's, or their friend's. They're "borrowing" Christianity for a while, perhaps because it meets a particular social or emotional need in their life at the moment, though they may not even realize it. It's like borrowing money or clothes from a friend, only to give it back when you're done with it or when it no longer serves its purpose anymore. They're "renters" and not yet full-fledged "owners." Maybe you've known someone who at one time was very committed to God while in junior or senior high only to jettison their faith and fall away later in high school or college! It is very likely that they never had a "faith of their own" to begin with. They may have been at church because their friends were there or came because their mom and dad brought them. But when their friends changed or when mom and dad were no longer around, their faith was cast aside. And this reveals the fact that they had never really owned that faith in the first place. It *could* indicate that they have never truly come into a saving relationship with Jesus. Only God really knows.

So how can someone know if they have come to "own their faith"? How can a person know the difference between "renting" someone else's faith and having a faith of their own?

The following is a checklist — a sort of personal inventory — to see just how much of your faith is really yours. Go through and check the ones that apply to you and your spiritual life.

"RENTERS" vs.	"OWNERS"
Apathetic/indifferent about spiritual things.	Eager to grow and learn. Wants to know more.
Enjoys the "shallow end" of Bible study.	Desires depth and more insight.
Externally motivated from the outside. Needs to have a "jump-start." Has to be "enticed" w/fun spiritual activities at church.	Motivated from the heart. Doesn't need to be "begged" to partici-pate in things.
Inconsistent. Sporadic. Casual commitment.	Faithful. Consistent. Can be counted on.
Has a "two-faced faith." One person at church and another at work / school / weekends.	Is genuine and real. Same person at all times.
Only interested in the benefits of Christianity. Asks, "What's in it for me?"	Interested in serving others. Asks, "How can I help someone else?"
Doesn't last. His/her faith fizzles out. Loses interest in spiritual things.	Keeps on going. Perseveres. Crosses over to the other side of the bridge.
Can't defend the faith.	Is trained to defend the faith.

Those are some of the differences between renting and owning your own faith. Of course, still being in the *process* of fully owning your faith doesn't mean you're a second-class Christian. To varying degrees, we are all continuing to grow, learn, and embrace God's Word at different levels.

What about you? Where are you on the "bridge"? This isn't just a journey confined to young people, as most Christian adults struggle in this area as well. Are you closer to the "renting" side or the "owning" side? Are you currently,

- progressing forward spiritually, moving backward, or standing still?

Pause for a moment before reading further and pray about those areas of faith you have yet to fully "own."

- Are there doctrines, truths, or passages in the Bible of which you remain skeptical? If so, then seek out answers.

- Is there a belief you are struggling with?

- An area of your life you're unwilling to give over to Christ?

- Do you fear walking across that bridge, afraid you won't do a good job "giving an answer" for your faith to your world?

- Do you feel like you're still "renting"?

- Are you secretly fearful unbelievers or your children will ask questions you can't answer?

- Do you have doubts because of your questions and you need those answers?

Talk to God about those areas and give them over to Him. Ask Him for His strength to deal with them. Ask, "Lord, what do I need to do in these areas of my life in order to move on toward maturity? What decisions do I need to make? What practical steps do I need to take? Who do I need to talk to? What resource should I consult?"

From the Inside Out

Jesus and Paul knew something that many pastors in America need to re-discover — that we cannot do something *for* God until God first does something *in* us. God desires to work in this generation before He works through them. And that's exactly what happens when we invest the Word of God into our young people. You can change a person's behavior through gimmicks, but you can only change a heart through the Holy Spirit and the Word of God.

Paul spent years establishing individuals and churches in their faith. He himself spent three years being privately grounded in truth by the

Holy Spirit (Gal. 1:11–17). Jesus spent three years helping His disciples own their faith. Though He spoke often to large crowds, the majority of His time and teaching was spent with just 12 men. To large crowds, He spoke primarily about salvation. But to His small group, the topic was discipleship — how to know God intimately and follow Him passionately. The Bible says Jesus chose these men that "they might be with him" (Mark 3:14). That's the heart of ministry — time together sharing our lives *and* God's Word with one another. Here then, in Paul's own words, is the biblical balance of discipleship:

> But we were gentle among you, like a nursing mother taking care of her own children. So, being affectionately desirous of you, we were *ready to share with you* not only the gospel of God but also our own selves, because you had become very dear to us (1 Thess. 2:7–8, emphasis added).

The "gospel of God" is the Word of God, the body of truth we know as the "faith," beginning in Genesis and ending in Revelation. That's the *content* of our apologetic. We do not redefine that truth, but rather teach it plainly and passionately. But it doesn't stop there. "Our own selves" refers to us imparting our lives in service to those whose spiritual care God has entrusted to us. That's the *character* of our apologetic.

Both are necessary for an effective transfer of faith. Content without character only makes people smarter. Character without content only gives a good example. To teach the Word outside the context of relationship often produces cold doctrine, lifeless truth, and a pharisaical sort of pride. But when life is shared *without* the Word, it produces superficiality, ignorance, and experientialism. We need both, producing a much needed balance. While *sharing* the truth, we at the same time *incarnate* it.

Aren't you glad God gave us this balance in our life and ministry? And the result?

Paul wrote to the Corinthians,

> You yourselves are our letter of recommendation, written on our hearts, to be known and read by all (2 Cor. 3:2).

In other words, those to whom we pass the baton become the *validation* of our lives and ministries. *Disciple making is a generational affair.* The glory of God in the next generation is *why* we do what we do. To see them grip the baton of faith and run with it is our highest reward. It makes everything we do worth all the toil and sacrifice. Therefore, we must make it a top priority to train, equip, mentor, and model an effective apologetic for this generation of young believers living in a post-modern world.

Jesus chose this approach to ministry because He knew it would make the greatest impact in their lives. And apparently it worked, because you and I are the glorious result of His men owning their faith!

Chapter 7

Jesus and the Ark

In the year this book is being written, Answers in Genesis is in the midst of constructing a life-size Noah's ark. As part of the due diligence in regard to this undertaking, ARG contracted a general population study to project attendance to "Ark Encounter." As a result of this study, ARG predicts a minimum of 1.4 million visitors to the structure in the first year.

In this study (of which 55 percent indicated they were regular church attendees), participants were asked, "Do you believe Noah's Ark was actually built or only a legend?" and 77 percent said it was actually built.

Concerning the building of a replica ark, ARG also discovered that only 11 percent said it was *not* a worthy idea; 68 percent said they would personally like to see the ark built; and 63 percent (that's approximately 200 million people in the USA alone) indicated they would likely visit the ark.

Obviously, there's a lot of interest in the topic of Noah's ark. However, in this same study, we discovered that the 20s generation is less sympathetic to the Christian worldview. For instance, when asked "Do you believe Noah's ark was actually built or only a legend?" the results for those who said yes were as follows:

60s — 86%
50s — 74%
40s — 81%
30s — 81%
20s — 52%

It's clear that the 20s generation is drifting away from believing the biblical account of the ark and the Flood. Of the people who regularly attend church, 89 percent of the 20s generation said they believe in Noah's ark and the Flood. But the 20s group in the general population, as discussed earlier, has continued drifting away from the Church, with a significant increase in the number who reject the biblical account of the ark and Flood. Though alarming, this comes as no surprise to those who are familiar with Scripture.

A Ship with No Anchor

One of the Apostle Paul's passions was preserving the purity of the Bride of Christ, the Church. In fact, most of his epistles were written to counteract false teaching and those who would threaten the integrity of the Word of God and the gospel of grace. Of particular importance is his prophetic warnings concerning the Church in the last days. Writing to Timothy, Paul predicted,

> Now the Spirit expressly says that in later times some will depart from the faith by devoting themselves to deceitful spirits and teachings of demons, through the insincerity of liars whose consciences are seared (1 Tim. 4:1–2).

And again, in his final letter to the young pastor,

> But understand this, that in the last days there will come times of difficulty. . . . having the appearance of godliness, but denying its power. Avoid such people (2 Tim. 3:1–5).

> But as for you, continue in what you have learned and have firmly believed, knowing from whom you learned it and how from childhood you have been acquainted with the sacred writ-

ings, which are able to make you wise for salvation through faith in Christ Jesus. All Scripture is breathed out by God and profitable for teaching, for reproof, for correction, and for training in righteousness, that the man of God may be complete, equipped for every good work (2 Tim. 3:14–17).

But where today do we see this "departing from the faith"? Are we currently living in the "times of difficulty" Paul wrote about? I believe we certainly are in a particular time of difficulty. At no time since before the Protestant Reformation has the integrity and teaching of God's Word been so questioned, misinterpreted, and maligned as it is today, particularly in regard to the Book of Genesis. When an arsonist burns a house down, he doesn't throw a match on the roof. Rather, he pours gasoline in the basement so the fire burns from the bottom up. The Book of Genesis is like a foundation to biblical structure.[1] Many core doctrines (directly or indirectly), including the gospel of Jesus Christ, are founded in Genesis 1–11. We also find the doctrine of marriage between a man and woman in Genesis 1 and 2 (later quoted by Jesus in Matthew 19:4–7). Therefore, to undermine Genesis, we subvert marriage itself, as well as the gospel, as the historical account of original sin and the resulting need for a Savior are outlined there.

Now in order to effectively discredit the historical veracity of the Bible, you would have to definitively disprove Scripture's record with undeniable facts, which of course, no one has been able to do in over 2,000 years. On the contrary, with every turn of the archeologist's spade, and the more we understand biology, geology, astronomy, and anthropology, the Bible is proven trustworthy over and over again — right from the very beginning. However, this certainly hasn't discouraged those ignorant of Scripture's impeccable track record from continually casting doubt on its account of humankind's history. One of the targeted areas secular evolutionary scientists attack vehemently is the testimony of the ark and the Great Flood. However, secularists have to denigrate the account of the Flood in order to do this, because if there really was a global Flood as the Bible describes, then the whole timeline

---

1. This is discussed in detail in the book *The Lie: Evolution* by Ken Ham (Green Forest, AR: Master Books, 1987).

of evolutionary geology collapses, imploding under its own weight. If Genesis is true, evolutionary thought is decimated.

Biblical creationist Dr. Terry Mortenson has conclusively documented how the idea of millions of years of time grew out of naturalism (atheism) in the late 18th and early 19th centuries.[2] They claim most of the fossil record was laid down over millions of years and was not the result of a catastrophic, global Flood. Only through millions of years can Darwin propose that changes were made in biology (e.g., adaptation/speciation etc.), enabling one kind of animal to change into a completely different kind of animal. This is their "molecules to man" evolutionary proposal.

Even though we know sin is the ultimate "disease problem" in this world, I liken the teaching of millions of years to a disease, with the teaching of evolution as a mere symptom of that disease.

The Real Reason Secularists Reject Noah

Most of the questions I get from the secular media concern the age of the earth or why we believe dinosaurs lived with people — not so much about evolution itself. I've found that if a Christian doesn't believe in evolution, secularists will scoff a bit. But if a Christian rejects millions of years, then they really go ballistic. They will call you anti-academic, anti-science, anti-intellectual, etc. This happens because millions of years is really the religion of this age used to justify explaining life without God.

You see, without millions of years, the secularists can't propose a molecules-to-man evolution. As one Nobel prize-winner, George Wald, said,

> Time is in fact the hero of the plot. . . . What we regard as impossible on the basis of human experience is meaningless here. Given so much time, the "impossible" becomes possible,

---

2. See his article, "Philosophical Naturalism and the Age of the Earth: Are They Related?" https://answersingenesis.org/age-of-the-earth/are-philosophical-naturalism-and-age-of-the-earth-related/, as well as his article "The Historical Development of the Old-Earth Geological Time-Scale," https://answersingenesis.org/age-of-the-earth/the-historical-development-of-the-old-earth-geological-time-scale/, his chapter 3 in Terry Mortenson and Thane H. Ury, eds., *Coming to Grips with Genesis* (Green Forest, AR: Master Books, 2008), and his book (a shortened version of his PhD thesis), *The Great Turning Point* (Green Forest, AR: Master Books, 2004).

the possible probable, and the probable virtually certain. One has only to wait: time itself performs the miracles.[3]

He also stated, ". . . the origin of life . . . However improbable we regard this event, or any of the steps which it involves, given enough time it will almost certainly happen at least once."[4]

If the earth is only *thousands* of years old (as calculated using the six days of creation and the genealogies in Scripture), then molecules-to-man evolution as Darwin discussed is logically and biologically impossible. Further, one cannot observe evolution, in the molecules-to-man sense, happening. Yes, we see changes in animals and plants, but those changes do not involve the addition of brand new genetic information as required by such an evolutionary process. Secularists have to have an incomprehensible amount of time (millions of years), to propose an incomprehensible process (molecules-to-man evolution).

Sadly, because secularism intimidates people to believe in millions of years, many Christians have adopted this pagan thinking and thus compromise God's Word, undermining its authority.

We have previously discussed that a fossil record involving millions of years would place death, bloodshed, disease, and thorns *before* man's sin — which is contrary to what the Bible teaches. But if the global Flood of Noah's day really did occur (about 4,300 years ago), then this would explain most of the fossil record, thus "washing away" the idea of millions of years! Therefore, the secularists *have* to oppose the idea that there was a global Flood, otherwise they cannot propose biological evolution! They also cannot allow each animal kind to be represented on an ark, as they insist the various species within these kinds evolved over millions of years.

For these reasons, I believe an apologetic for the ark and Global Flood narrative is not only necessary, but also increasingly relevant for this generation.

Think about it. You rarely hear of secularists attacking the account of Samson killing 300 Philistines? Or Elijah and the prophets of Baal?

---

3. George Wald, "The Origin of Life," *Scientific American* 191, no. 48 (August 1954).
4. George Wald, "The Origin of Life," *A Treasury of Science*, 4th Rev. Ed., Harlow Shapley et al., eds. (New York: Harper and Brothers Publishers, 1958), p. 311.

Or Jesus walking on water? I believe this is because atheistic secularists and scientists do not see these biblical accounts as a threat to their belief system. In other words, whether there really was a "Samson" is not as big of a concern because, in their view, his account has little to do with mankind and world history. However, a catastrophic worldwide flood that altered continents, the topography of the planet, and destroyed every land animal (except those on the ark) . . . well *that* kind of account gets their attention! The Flood messes with not only their "official" version of earth's historical record, but also threatens their very worldview!

If the Flood really happened as Scripture claims it did, then everything secular and evolutionary scientists, geologists, and anthropologists have believed for over 100 years is suddenly transformed into a glorified fairy tale for adults. And that would make both them and an entire body of thought irrelevant, meaningless, and worthless. In other words, they would be considered fools.

And they can't have that, now, can they?

Therefore, they continue in their relentless attack on the credibility and claims of Scripture as it relates to the Flood.

But even for those who profess belief in Scripture, the story of the ark and the Flood raises many questions, which when left unanswered, tend to also raise the *Christian's* doubt level. To be clear, the credibility of the Flood event has a huge impact on how people view the rest of Scripture. So let's address some of the most-often asked questions concerning the ark and the Flood that I have been asked from inside and outside the Church. If such questions remain unanswered, this can be a major contributing factor to why so many in the 20s generation have left (and are leaving) the Church. Answering them is part of equipping believers with a reasonable apologetic concerning the ark and Flood. So here are some of those questions:

- How large was Noah's ark?

- Could Noah have built the ark, and if so, how?

- How could Noah have rounded up so many animals?

- Were dinosaurs on the ark?

- Could all those animals fit on one boat?

- How did he care for the animals for over a year?

- Could the ark really survive such a violent flood?

- Where did all the water come from? And where did it go afterward?

- Was the Flood really global, or merely regional?

- Where is the evidence for such a Flood?

- Where is Noah's ark today?

- Why is the ark so important to Christians?

- What are the theological problems with denying the ark account?

- How did Jesus and the New Testament authors understand the Flood account?

- Is there credible extra-biblical evidence for the Flood?

- What are the spiritual implications of dismissing the Flood as myth?

How Large Was Noah's Ark?

Unlike many whimsical drawings that depict the ark as some kind of overgrown houseboat (with giraffes sticking out the top), the ark described in the Bible was a huge seaworthy vessel. In fact, not until the late 1800s was a ship built that exceeded the capacity of Noah's ark.

The dimensions of the ark are convincing for two reasons: the proportions are like that of a modern cargo ship, and it is about as large as a wooden ship can be built. The cubit gives us a good indication of size.[5]

After much research, Answers in Genesis is using a 20.4-inch cubit. There are several articles about cubits on the worldwideflood.com website.

---

5. The cubit was defined as the length of the forearm from elbow to fingertip. Ancient cubits vary anywhere from 17.5 inches (45 cm) to 22 inches (56 cm), the longer sizes dominating the major ancient constructions. Despite this, even a conservative 18-inch (46 cm) cubit describes a sizeable vessel.

Our main researcher on this topic argues for using a royal cubit.[6] His rationale is based on the following reasons.

Royal cubits were often used in monumental structures throughout the Ancient Near East, indicating that the people may have been a little taller than evolutionists usually assert.[7]

The smaller cubits (17.5–18 inches) are often chosen to simply give a worst-case scenario for the size of the ark to hold the animals rather than a careful study of ancient cubits.

So assuming that a 20.4-inch cubit was actually Noah's cubit, then Noah was roughly 6'3" tall. This would mean that for the Ark Encounter project, the life-size ark will be 510 feet long, 85 feet wide, and 51 feet high.

In the Western world, wooden sailing ships never got much longer than about 330 feet (100 m), yet the ancient Greeks built vessels at least this size 2,000 years earlier. China built huge wooden ships in the 1400s that may have been as large as the ark. Thus, the biblical ark is one of the largest wooden ships of all time. Our life-size ark project in Kentucky shows the feasibility of such a wooden ship. For more information go to www.arkencounter.com.

How Could Noah Build the Ark?

Scripture doesn't specifically tell us Noah and his sons built the ark by themselves. Noah could have hired skilled laborers or had relatives help build the vessel. However, nothing indicates that they could not — or that they did not — build the ark themselves in the time allotted. The physical strength and mental processes of men in Noah's day was at least as great (quite likely, even much superior) to our own.[8] The genius of ancient man certainly would have had efficient means for harvesting and cutting timber, as well as for shaping, transporting, and erecting the massive beams and boards required.

---

6. http://worldwideflood.org/ark/noahs_cubit/cubit_paper.htm.
7. The cubit described in Ezekiel 40:5 is a cubit and a handbreadth, perhaps indicating that the original cubit was longer than the cubit that would be popular at the time Ezekiel described. Our researcher cites a reference that puts this cubit at 20.4 inches.
8. For the evidence, see Dr. Donald Chittick, *The Puzzle of Ancient Man* (Newberg, OR: Creation Compass, 1998). This book details evidence of man's intelligence in early post-Flood civilizations.

Today, one or two men can erect a large house in just 12 weeks. How much more could three or four men do in a few years? Noah's generation was making complex musical instruments, forging metal, and building cities, so their tools, machines, and techniques were not as primitive as many might imagine. History has also shown that technology can be lost. In Egypt, China, and the Americas, earlier dynasties built impressive buildings and were skilled in fine art and science. Many so-called modern inventions, like concrete, turn out to be re-inventions that were used by the Romans. Even early post-Flood civilizations display all the engineering know-how necessary for a project like Noah's ark. People sawing and drilling wood in Noah's day, only a few centuries before the Egyptians were sawing and drilling granite, is very reasonable! The idea that early civilizations were primitive and unskilled is an evolutionary concept. And sadly, even many Christians tend to think in an "evolutionary" way about the past — that humans weren't as intelligent or didn't have advanced technology at the time of Noah.

In reality, when God created Adam, he was perfect. Today, the individual human intellect has suffered from 6,000 years of sin and decay. The sudden rise in technology in the last few centuries has nothing to do with increasing intelligence; it is a combination of publishing and sharing ideas, and the spread of key inventions that became tools for investigation and manufacturing. One of the most recent tools is the computer, which in reality compensates a great deal for our natural decline in mental performance and discipline, while also permitting us to gather and store information as perhaps never before.

How Could Noah Round Up So Many Animals?

Genesis 6:20 tells us that Noah didn't have to search or travel to far away places to bring the animals on board. Consider that the world map was completely different before the Flood, and on the basis of Genesis 1, there might have been only one continent. The animals simply arrived at the ark as if called by a "homing instinct" (a behavior implanted in the animals by their Creator). However He did it, according to Scripture it was God who brought the animals to Noah.

Though this was no doubt a supernatural event (one that cannot be explained by our understanding of nature), compare it to the impressive migratory behavior we see in some animals today. We are still far from understanding all the marvelous animal behaviors exhibited in God's creation: the migration of Canadian geese and other birds, the amazing flights of monarch butterflies, the annual travels of whales and fish, hibernation instincts, earthquake sensitivity, and countless other fascinating capabilities of God's animal kingdom. So to claim that so many could not have come to the ark is a faulty conclusion.

Were Dinosaurs on Noah's Ark?

This is one of the questions most often asked of me. The history of God's creation (told in Genesis 1 and 2) tells us that all the land-dwelling creatures were made on day 6 of creation week — the same day God made Adam and Eve. Therefore, dinosaurs (being land animals) were clearly made with man. Keep in mind the word "dinosaur" was only invented in 1841 as a name for a particular group of land animals.

Also, two of every kind (seven of some) of land animal (which must have included the dinosaur kinds) boarded the ark. The description of "behemoth" in chapter 40 of the Book of Job (Job lived after the Flood) seems to fit with something like a sauropod dinosaur. The ancestor of "behemoth" must have been on board the ark.[9]

Additionally, we also find many dinosaurs that were trapped and fossilized in Flood sediment. And just as the numerous Flood legends point back to the real Flood of Noah's day, creationists believe the many dragon legends could be the result of encounters with real creatures, perhaps even what we today call dinosaurs. The only way this could happen is if dinosaurs were on the ark.

Juveniles of even the largest land animals do not present a size problem, and, being young, they have their full breeding life ahead of them. Yet most dinosaurs were not very large at all — some were the size of a chicken (although absolutely no relation to birds, as many evolutionists

---

9. For some remarkable evidence that dinosaurs have lived until relatively recent times, see chapter 12, "What Really Happened to the Dinosaurs?" Also read *The Great Dinosaur Mystery Solved* (Green Forest, AR: New Leaf Press, 2000). Also visit www.answersingenesis.org/go/dinosaurs.

claim). Most scientists agree that the average size of a dinosaur is actually the size of a bison. So God most likely brought Noah two young adult sauropods (e.g., apatosaurs), rather than two full-grown sauropods. The same goes for elephants, giraffes, and other animals that grow to be very large, even though there was adequate room for most fully-grown adult animals anyway.

It should also be noted that, although there are hundreds of names for different varieties (species) of dinosaurs that have been discovered, there are probably only about 50 different kinds, because there are only around 50 families of dinosaurs.

How Could Noah Fit All the Animals on the Ark?

First of all, the ark did not need to carry every kind of animal — nor did God command it. It carried only air-breathing, land-dwelling creatures. Aquatic life (fish, whales, etc.) survived outside the ark (although the variety we observe today makes it obvious that many did not survive the Flood). This cuts down significantly the total number of animals that needed to be on board.

Another factor greatly reducing the space requirements is the fact that the tremendous variety in species we see today did not exist in the days of Noah. Our researchers (in preparation for the life-size ark project), on the basis of which animals have been documented to breed together, believe that the Hebrew word for "kind," in most instances, is equivalent to the "family" level in mans' classification system. So only the parent "kinds" of the various species of land creatures were required to be on board in order to repopulate the earth.[10] For example, only two dogs (there is one dog family), were needed to give rise to all the dog species that exist today. Our researchers believe the number of actual

---

10. For example: more than 200 different breeds of dogs exist today, from the miniature poodle to the St. Bernard — all of which have descended from one original dog "kind" (as have the wolf, dingo, etc.). Many other types of animals — cat kind, horse kind, cow kind, etc. — have similarly been naturally and selectively bred to achieve the wonderful variation in species that we have today. God "programmed" variety into the genetic code of all animal kinds — even humankind! God also made it impossible for the basic "kinds" of animals to breed and reproduce with each other. For example, cats and dogs cannot breed to make a new type of creature. This is by God's design, and it is one fact that makes evolution impossible.

kinds needed on the ark could be as low as 1,000, but up to 1,500 (using fossil evidence that is very fragmentary). Also, there is debate as to whether those that went on the ark in sevens means seven pairs or seven individuals. So the number of land animals needed on the ark could be as low as 3,000 (or even less) or as high as 7,000 (which is probably way too high an estimation). Most land animals are not that large. The point is, when considering the size of the ark there was plenty of room for all the land animal kinds.

We would conclude that much less than half of the cumulative area of the ark's three decks were needed for the animals. This meant there was plenty of storage room for fresh food, water, and lodging for Noah and his family.

How Did Noah Care for All the Animals?

Just as God brought the animals to Noah by some form of supernatural means, He surely also prepared them for this amazing event. Creation scientists suggest that God gave the animals the ability to hibernate, as we see in many species today. Most animals react to natural disasters in ways that were designed to help them survive, so it's very possible many animals did hibernate, perhaps even supernaturally intensified by God.

There could also have simply been a normal response to the darkness and confinement of a rocking ship, as the fact that God told Noah to build rooms ("*qen*" — literally, in Hebrew, "nests") in Genesis 6:14 implies that the animals were subdued or nesting. God also told Noah to take food for them (Genesis 6:21), which tells us that they were not in a year-long coma.

If we could walk through the ark as it was being built, we would undoubtedly be amazed at the ingenious systems on board for water and food storage and distribution. As Woodmorappe explains in *Noah's Ark: A Feasibility Study*,[11] a small group of farmers today can raise thousands of cattle and other animals in a very small space. One can easily imagine all kinds of devices on the ark that would have enabled a small number of people to feed and care for the animals, from watering to waste removal.

---

11. John Woodmorappe, *Noah's Ark: A Feasibility Study* (Santee, CA: Institute for Creation Research, 1996).

It's entirely possible for Noah to have constructed a plumbing system for gravity-fed drinking water, a ventilation system driven by wind or wave motion, or hoppers that dispense grain as the animals eat it. *None* of these require higher technology than what we know existed in ancient cultures.

How Could a Flood Destroy Every Living Thing?

Scripture claims that every thing that breathed on land was killed in the Flood (Genesis 7:21–22). Noah's Flood was much more destructive than a massive rainstorm ever could be, as the "fountains of the great deep" also broke open, as well as rain. In other words, earthquakes, volcanoes, and geysers of molten lava and scalding water were squeezed out of the earth's crust in a violent, explosive upheaval. These fountains were not stopped until 150 days into the Flood — so the earth was literally churning underneath the waters for about five months! (Gen. 7:24). Then the Floodwaters ran off the earth into the oceans. Psalm 104 possibly indicates how God ended the Flood, by raising the mountains and lowering the ocean basis. This produced more catastrophic events that shaped the earth's surface. The Flood's duration was extensive, and Noah and his family were aboard the ark for approximately a year (Gen. 7:11, 8:14–16).

Relatively recent local floods, volcanoes, and earthquakes — though clearly devastating to life and land — are tiny in comparison to the worldwide catastrophe that destroyed "the world that then existed" (2 Peter 3:6). All land animals and people not on board the ark were destroyed in the floodwaters, with billions of creatures preserved in the great fossil record we see today.

Could the Ark Really Survive Such a Violent Flood?

For many years, biblical creationists have simply depicted the ark as a rectangular box, helping to accentuate its size. It also explained its capacity, illustrating how easily the ark could have handled the payload. With the rectangular shape, the ark's stability against rolling could be demonstrated by simple calculations.

However, the Bible does not say the ark was a rectangular box. In fact, Scripture does not elaborate about the shape of Noah's ark beyond those superb, overall proportions — length, breadth, and depth. Ships have long been described like this without implying a block-shaped hull.

Noah's ark was the focus of a major 1993 scientific study headed by Dr. Seon Hong at the world-class ship research center KRISO, based in Daejeon, South Korea.[12] Dr. Hong's team compared 12 hulls of different proportions to discover which design was most practical. No hull shape was found to significantly outperform the 4,300-year-old biblical design. In fact, the ark's careful balance is easily lost if the proportions are modified, rendering the vessel either unstable, prone to fracture, or dangerously uncomfortable.

The research team found that the proportions of Noah's ark carefully balanced the conflicting demands of stability (resistance to capsizing), comfort ("seakeeping"), and strength. In fact, the ark has the same proportions as a modern cargo ship.

The study also confirmed that the ark could handle waves as high as 100 feet (30 m). Dr. Hong is now director general of KRISO and claims "life came from the sea," obviously not the words of a creationist on a mission to promote the worldwide Flood. Endorsing the seaworthiness of Noah's ark obviously did not damage Dr. Hong's credibility.[13]

In Hebrew, "Ark" is the obscure term *tebah*, a word that appears only one other time in the Bible, describing the basket that carried the infant Moses (Exodus 2:3). One was a huge, wooden ship and the other a tiny, wicker basket. Both floated, both preserved life, and both were covered; but the similarity ends there. If the word implied anything about shape, it would be "an Egyptian basket-like shape," typically rounded. More likely, however, *tebah* means something else, like "lifeboat."

The Bible leaves the details regarding the shape of the ark wide open — anything from a rectangular box with hard right angles and no curvature at all, to a ship-like form. Box-like has the largest carrying capacity, but a ship-like design would be safer and more comfortable in heavy

---

12. Dr. Seon Won Hong was principal research scientist when he headed up the Noah's ark investigation. In May 2005 Dr. Hong was appointed director general of MOERI (formerly KRISO). Dr. Hong earned a B.S. degree in naval architecture from Seoul National University and a Ph.D. degree in applied mechanics from the University of Michigan, Ann Arbor.

13. worldwideflood.com/ark/hull_form/hull_optimization.htm.

seas. Such discussion is irrelevant if God intended to sustain the ark no matter how well designed and executed.[14]

Was Noah's Flood Global?

> And the waters prevailed so mightily on the earth that all the high mountains under the whole heaven were covered. The waters prevailed above the mountains, covering them fifteen cubits deep (Gen. 7:19–20).

Many Christians today claim that Noah's Flood was only a local phenomenon. They generally believe this because they've accepted the evolutionary history of the earth, which interprets fossil layers as the history of the sequential appearance of life over millions of years.[15] At one time, scientists understood the fossils, which are buried in water-carried sediments of mud and sand, to be mostly the result of the Great Flood. Those who now accept millions of years of gradual accumulation of fossils think they have explained away the evidence for the global Flood. However, the evidence says otherwise.

First, if the Flood only affected the area of Mesopotamia, as some claim, why did Noah have to build an ark? He could have simply walked to the other side of the mountains and escaped. Additionally, if the Flood were local, people not living in the vicinity of the Flood would not have been affected by it, and thus escaped God's judgment on sin.

In 2 Peter 3, the coming global judgment by fire is likened to the former judgment by water in Noah's Flood. A partial judgment in Noah's day, therefore, would mean a partial judgment in the future.

Second, if the Flood were only local, how could the waters rise to 20 feet (6 m) above the mountains (Gen. 7:20)? Water seeks its own level; it could not have risen to cover the local mountains while leaving the rest of the world untouched.

---

14. Based on additional research, Answers in Genesis has designed aspects of the life-size ark as part of the Ark Encounter project, including a bow and a wooden "sail" as seen on ancient ships. Such structures help with stability for such a vessel.

15. For compelling evidence that the earth is not billions of years old, read *The Young Earth* by Dr. John Morris (Green Forest, AR: Master Books, 1994), and *Thousands . . . not Billions* by Dr. Don DeYoung (Green Forest, AR: Master Books, 2005); also see www.answersingenesis.org/go/young.

Even what is now Mt. Everest was once covered with water and then uplifted afterward.[16] Again, if we even out the ocean basins and flatten out the mountains, there's enough water to cover the entire earth by about 1.7 miles (2.7 km).[17] The ark would not have been riding at the current height of Mt. Everest, thus no lack of oxygen at high altitudes for Noah.

Third, if the Flood were local, God would have repeatedly broken His promise never to send such a flood again. God put a rainbow in the sky as a covenant between God and man and the animals that He would never repeat such an event. But there have been huge local floods in recent times (e.g., in Bangladesh).

Obviously, if the Flood of Noah were only local in extent and because we have seen lots of local floods since Noah's day that have destroyed both man and animals, God has broken His promise many times over! To the contrary, this rainbow covenant God made with Noah and his descendants could only have been kept by God if the Flood were global in extent, because never since in human history has a global flood been experienced.

Fourth, if the Flood were only local in extent, why did Noah have to take birds on board the ark (Gen. 7:8), when the birds in that local flooded area could simply have flown away to safe unflooded areas? Similarly, why would Noah need to take animals on board the ark from his local area, when other representatives of those same animal kinds would surely have survived in other, unflooded areas?

Fifth, if it was only a local flood, why would Noah have had to build the ark on such a large scale as described above. Obviously, an ark of such dimensions would only be required if the Flood were global in extent, designed by God to destroy all land animals around the world, except for those preserved on that ark. Indeed, God could have simply

---

16. Mount Everest is more than 5 miles (8 km) high. How, then, could the Flood have covered "all the mountains under the whole heaven"? Before the Flood, the mountains were not so high. The mountains today were formed only toward the end of, and after, the Flood by collision of the tectonic plates and the associated up-thrusting. In support of this, the layers that form the uppermost parts of Mt. Everest are themselves composed of fossil-bearing, water-deposited layers.

17. A.R. Wallace, *Man's Place in the Universe* (New York: McClure, Phillips & Co, 1903), p. 225–226; www.wku.edu/~smithch/wallace/S728-3.htm.

told Noah and his family to migrate with any required animals and birds out of the area that was going to be flooded.

Where Is the Evidence for Such a Flood?

> For they deliberately overlook this fact, that the heavens existed long ago, and the earth was formed out of water and through water by the word of God, and that by means of these the world that then existed was deluged with water and perished (2 Pet. 3:5–6).

Evidence of Noah's Flood can be seen all over the earth, from seabeds to mountaintops. Wherever you go, the physical features of the earth's terrain clearly indicate a catastrophic past, from canyons and craters to coal beds and caverns. Some layers of strata extend across continents, revealing the effects of a huge catastrophe. The earth's crust has massive amounts of layered sedimentary rock, sometimes miles deep! These layers of sand, soil, and material — mostly laid down by water — were once soft like mud, but they are now hard stone. Encased in these sedimentary layers are billions of dead things (fossils of plants and animals) buried *very quickly*. The evidence all over the earth is staring everyone in the face.

Where Is Noah's Ark Today?

Scripture says Noah's ark rested "on the mountains of Ararat" (Gen. 8:4). The location of these mountains could refer to several areas in the Middle East, such as Mt. Ararat in Turkey or other mountain ranges in neighboring countries. Mt. Ararat has attracted the most attention because it has permanent ice, and there have been reports of supposed past sightings of the ark there. But though many expeditions have searched for the ark, there remains no conclusive evidence of the ark's location or survival. Considering it landed about 4,300 years ago, the ark could easily have deteriorated, been destroyed, or been used as lumber by Noah and his descendants.

Some Christians believe the ark could indeed be preserved — perhaps to be providentially revealed at a future time as a reminder of the past judgment and the judgment to come. However, this is not prophesied in Scripture, and such discoveries may not be as convincing as one may think. Jesus said, "If they do not hear Moses and the Prophets, neither will they be convinced if someone rise from the dead" (Luke 16:31).

Why Is the Ark So Important to Christians?

As God's Son, the Lord Jesus Christ is like Noah's ark. Jesus came to seek and to save the lost (Luke 19:10). Just as Noah and his family were saved by the ark and rescued by God from the floodwaters, so anyone who believes in Jesus as Lord and Savior will be spared from the coming final judgment of mankind, rescued by God from the fire that will destroy the earth after the last days (2 Pet. 3:7). Noah and his family had to go through a doorway into the ark to be saved, and the Lord shut the door behind them (Gen. 7:16). So we too have to go through a "doorway" to be saved so that we won't be eternally separated from God. The Son of God, Jesus, stepped into history to pay the penalty for our sin of rebellion. Jesus said, "I am the door. If anyone enters by me, he will be saved and will go in and out and find pasture" (John 10:9).

What Are the Theological Problems with Denying the Ark Account?

Those Christians who accept an evolutionary timeframe, with its fossil accumulation, also rob the Fall of Adam of its serious consequences. Chronologically, they put fossils (which testify of disease, suffering, and death) *before* Adam and Eve sinned and brought death and suffering into the world. By doing this, they also unknowingly undermine the meaning of the death and Resurrection of Christ. Such a scenario also robs all meaning from God's description of His finished creation as "very good."

For the evolutionist, fossil-bearing sedimentary layers were laid down over millions of years *preceding* the appearance of man on earth, including Adam. So for a Christian to accept the millions of years scenario means that animals were living, dying, suffering disease, eating each other, and being buried and fossilized *prior* to Adam's appearance in the Garden of Eden. In the geologic record we find the fossilized remains of fish eating other fish, animals eating other animals, animals with diseases like cancer, and much more, which indicates that these fossils are a record of disease, violence, carnivory, and death.

This presents a huge theological problem. In Genesis 1:30–31 we are told that when God created all the animals they all were vegetarians, and that God was pleased with everything that He had created because it was "very good." This means all of creation was perfect.

But according to the Bible, it is not until *after* God pronounced the Curse on all of creation because of Adam and Eve's disobedience that we are told the ground would bring forth thorns and thistles (Gen. 3:17–18). Evolutionary geologists claim there are fossilized thorns in Canadian sedimentary layers that are supposedly 400 million years old.[18] Those who believe the Bible cannot accept this age-claim however.

If God's Word is true, then these fossilized thorns could only have grown *after* the Curse, *after* Adam was created by God. So the geologic record in which these fossilized thorns are found could *only* have been deposited after the Curse. However, the only event after the Curse that could have been responsible for burying and fossilizing these thorns, and most of the billions of other plants and animals we see in the vast rock layers of the earth, is the yearlong Genesis Flood. This effectively rules out millions of years claimed by evolution.

How Did Jesus and the New Testament Authors Understand the Flood Account?

Jesus made special reference to Noah and the Flood in Luke 17:26–30, where He said that, "the flood came and destroyed them all." Further, Jesus describes the Flood and all the ungodly being destroyed by it, comparing it to a parallel future judgment. Again, if the coming judgment is global, then so was the former judgment. In addition, there is nothing to indicate Jesus understood God's Flood judgment to be anything other than global.

Paul believed in the accuracy and historicity of the Old Testament record. He even compares the literal existence of Jesus to the literal existence of the one man, Adam (Rom. 5:12–21). This scenario is impossible under evolutionary thought.

Similarly, the Apostle Peter in 2 Peter 3:3–7 warned of last-days scoffers who would willfully forget that after the earth was created by God, once flooded with water, and that the present earth is "stored up

---

18. W.N. Stewart and G.W. Rothwell, *Paleobotany and the Evolution of Plants* (Cambridge, UK: Cambridge University Press, 1993), p. 172–176.

for fire . . . until the day of judgment." There are three events he is thus referring to: the creation of the world (Greek *kosmos*), the destruction of that world (Greek *kosmos*) by a watery cataclysm (the Flood), and the coming destruction of the heavens and the earth by fire in the future.

In context, it's clear Peter is teaching a literal, global Flood. Indeed, the use of the Greek term *kosmos* for both the world that was created and the world that was flooded leave no doubt as to his intended meaning.

Is There Credible Extra-biblical Evidence for the Flood?

The world teaches that the vast majority of the rock layers were laid down slowly over millions of years; but in light of a global Flood in Genesis 6–9, it makes more sense that the bulk of the rock layers that contain fossils were laid down during this catastrophe only thousands of years ago.

On the other hand, the description of the Flood in Genesis 6–8 is not hard to understand. We are told that the "fountains of the great deep" burst open and poured water out onto the earth's surface for 150 days (five months). Simultaneously, and for the same length of time, the "floodgates of heaven" were open, producing torrential global rainfall.[19]

The combined result was that the waters destructively rose across the face of the earth to eventually cover "*all* the high hills under the *whole* heaven." The mountains also were eventually covered, so that every creature "in whose nostrils is the breath of life" perished. If the Flood occurred, we should expect to find evidence today of billions of dead animals and plants buried in rock layers composed of water-deposited sand, lime, and mud all around the earth. And indeed, that's exactly what we do find — billions of fossils of animals and plants buried in sedimentary rock layers stretching across every continent all around the globe.[20] So the evidence is consistent with the biblical record. Millions of years are

---

19. The reference to 40 days and 40 nights (Gen. 7:12, 17) appears to be telling us how long it was before the ark started to float, for the windows of heaven were closed on the same day (150th) as the fountains of the deep were (Gen. 7:24–8:3). For a detailed argument based on the Hebrew text, see William Barrick, "Noah's Flood and Its Geological Implications," in Terry Mortenson and Thane H. Ury, eds., *Coming to Grips with Genesis* (Green Forest, AR: Master Books, 2008), p. 251–282.

20. See Ken Ham, ed., *The New Answers Book 3* (Green Forest, AR: Master Books, 2010), ch 29, Andrew A. Snelling, "What Are Some of the Best Flood Evidences?"

not necessary to form fossil-bearing sedimentary rock layers, as seen in the walls of the Grand Canyon and elsewhere, and could have formed rapidly during the year long catastrophic Flood of Noah.[21]

It should immediately be obvious that these two interpretations of the fossil evidence are mutually exclusive! Most of these rock layers are either the sobering testimony to Noah's Flood or the record of millions of years of history on this earth. One must be true and the other must be false. We can't consistently or logically believe in both, because the millions of years can't be fitted into the approximately year-long global cataclysmic Flood of Noah described in Genesis 6–8.

What Are the Spiritual Implications of Dismissing the Flood as Myth?

How do we establish beyond a doubt the details of an event that supposedly happened in the past? One way is to find witnesses who were there, or look for records written by witnesses. The Bible claims that God moved men through His Spirit to write down His words, and that they are not just the words of men but the Word of God (1 Thess. 2:13; 2 Pet. 1:20–21). The Book of Genesis claims to be the records from God telling us of the events of creation and of other events in this world's early history that have great bearing upon our present circumstances. Thus, the present is *not* the key to the past, as evolutionists claim. Rather, *revelation* is the key to the past.

The revelation in Genesis tells us about such events as creation, Noah's Flood, and the Tower of Babel. These are events that have made the earth's geology, geography, biology, etc., what they are today. Therefore, it's also true that what happened in the past is the key to the present. The entrance of sin into the world explains why we have death and mistakes occurring in our genes. The global devastation caused by Noah's Flood helps to explain the fossil record. The events at the Tower of Babel help us to come to an understanding of the origin of the different nations and cultures around the world.

---

21. Some localized fossil-bearing deposits may have formed after the Fall of Adam and Eve in sin and before Noah's Flood, and some of the localized fossiliferous rock layers at the top of the geological record were formed in post-Flood events. But creationist geologists are in general agreement that most of the fossil-bearing sedimentary rock record is a result of Noah's Flood.

Today, evolutionists deny that the biblical record can be taken seriously. They put their faith in their belief that "all things continue as they have done from the beginning," fulfilling the prophecy in 2 Peter 3.

Peter's prophecy tells us that men will deliberately reject three things:

1. That God created the world, which at first was covered with water (which means its surface was *cool* at the beginning, not a molten blob, as evolutionists teach).

2. That God once judged this world with a global, cataclysmic flood in Noah's time.

3. That God is going to judge this world again, only this time with fire.

People often make the statement, "If there is so much evidence that God created the world and sent a global cataclysmic flood, then surely all scientists would believe this." But Peter explains that it's not simply a matter of providing evidence to convince people, because people do not *want* to be convinced (2 Pet. 3:5). Romans 1:20 says there's enough evidence to convince everyone that God is Creator, so much so that we are condemned if we do not believe. Furthermore, Romans 1:18 tells us that men "by their unrighteousness suppress the truth." So it's not a matter of lack of evidence to convince people that the Bible is true; the problem is that they do not *want* to believe the Bible, and thus have closed their minds to truth. The reason for this is obvious. If people believed in the God of the Bible, they would have to acknowledge His authority and submit to Him. However, every human being suffers from the same problem — the sin which Adam committed in the Garden of Eden — a "disease" which we all inherit. Adam's sin was rebellion against God's authority. Likewise, people everywhere today are in rebellion against God, so to admit that the Bible is true would be an admission of their own sinful and rebellious nature and of their need to be born again through Christ.

It is easy to see this "willing ignorance" in action when watching debates over the creation/evolution issue. In most cases, the evolutionists are not interested in the wealth of data, evidence, and information the creationists put forward. Instead, they typically try to attack creationists by attempting to destroy their credibility. They're not interested in data, logical reasoning, or any evidence pointing to creation or refuting evolution, because they are totally committed to their religious faith in evolution.

For evolutionists to accept the facts presented by creationists would mean admitting the Bible is right, and thus the whole of their evolutionary philosophy would have to be rejected. *That's* what being "willingly ignorant" means.

Further, if they conceded that the Bible was true, they would have to agree with Jesus Christ, who uses the event of Noah's Flood as a warning that God has judged the earth, and will judge it again (Matt. 24:37–39). They would have to agree that God is going to come back as judge. The next time He will use fire as the method of judgment rather than water. Sinful man in rebellion against God does not want to admit that he must stand before the God of creation one day and account for his life. Thus, in rejecting creation and Noah's Flood, and claiming "scientific" evidence that supposedly supports his own belief, he becomes comfortable in not thinking about the coming judgment.

The late Isaac Asimov, an active anti-creationist, gave warnings about creationists. He was quoted as saying (in regard to creationists getting equal time for presenting the creation model in school), it is "today equal time, tomorrow the world."[22] Isaac Asimov was right! We are out to convince the world that Jesus Christ is Creator. Isaac Asimov was one who signed the Humanist Manifesto — he was out to convince the world that Jesus Christ is *not* the Creator.

We are out to convince people like Isaac Asimov that Jesus Christ is Creator. Why? Because we want a good fight? Because we like controversy? No, because we know that those who do not trust the Lord will spend eternity separated from Him.

And that is the ultimate purpose of any good apologetic (defense) — to convince someone of the truth and reasonable nature of the gospel. For all these reasons we've discussed, every believer should be acquainted with the overwhelming evidence concerning the ark and the Flood.

---

22. Isaac Asimov, *The Roving Mind* (Buffalo, NY: Prometheus Books, 1983), p. 19.

Failing to do so represents a departure from historic faith, and is an insult to the very God who claims His Word *is* "truth" (John 17:17).

So why all this information regarding the ark? The reason is that once belief in the ark and Genesis has eroded or been compromised, people are less likely to trust the rest of Scripture. These are foundational issues, not peripheral ones. I strongly believe that if general Bible and creation apologetics had been taught consistently in churches and Christian homes, we would likely not be seeing the 20s generation drift and depart from God as they have. So is there anything we can do to help undo what has happened?

Chapter 8

Already Too Late?

Lightning Strikes and Lava Flows

Some things in life happen in an instant — a car accident, a heart attack, or a lightning strike. They are sudden, immediate, and can change life as we know it. But other things in life happen gradually. Their impact is not glaring or obvious, but they nevertheless change things — sometimes dramatically. They move, not with giant steps, but rather incrementally. Like a slow-moving lava flow, they creep by the inch, bringing radical change to the landscape.

When it comes to a nation's spirituality and morality, change is typically more like a lava flow than a lightning strike. To the average citizen, these changes largely go unnoticed as they are small and seemingly insignificant. But then this change reaches a critical juncture, and catastrophic change ensues. I believe we are at that point in America — even in the whole Western world. And when it comes to morality, change is a critical component of Satan's evil agenda. And in the absence of moral leadership, there is virtually no way to impede the infringing flow of godlessness.

In the Book of Judges, twice we read what happens when there is no human authority to enforce what is right and wrong according to God's Word. In what is one of the saddest verses in all of Scripture, Joshua writes,

> In those days there was no king in Israel. Everyone did what was right in his own eyes (Judg. 17:6, 21:25).

This verse aptly spells out what we see happening in our own American culture. As I've said many times before, when a culture no longer builds its worldview on the foundation of the absolute authority of the Word of God, then increasingly people will want to do what is "right" in their own eyes. Eventually we reach a tipping point, a twisted perspective where, like Israel, we "call evil good and good evil," becoming those who "put darkness for light and light for darkness" (Isa. 5:20). Sadly, this is not just occurring outside the Church, but inside also.

Perhaps in no other area of society and morality are we seeing this happening than in the acceptance and legalization of same sex marriage. As gay "marriage" has been condoned and progressively legalized across this nation — from the U.S. president to individual states — there has been an increase in people justifying any relationship they desire, and defining marriage however they please. Since the Supreme Court of the United States has ruled in favor of gay "marriage," as I have said many times, we will also see polygamists clamoring to demand the legalization of polygamy as well.

To that point, the *New York Times* reported on a recent case in Utah with this headline:

A Utah Law Prohibiting Polygamy Is Weakened

The article begins this way:

> A federal judge has struck down parts of Utah's anti-polygamy law as unconstitutional in a case brought by a polygamous star of a reality television series. Months after the Supreme Court bolstered rights of same-sex couples, the Utah case could open a new frontier in the nation's recognition of once-prohibited relationships.[1]

Similarly, Jillian Keenan is an independent journalist who has contributed to *The New York Times* and the *Washington Post*. Earlier this year she wrote an article that contained the following:

---

1. www.nytimes.com/2013/12/15/us/a-utah-law-prohibiting-polygamy-is-weakened. html?_r=0.

While the Supreme Court and the rest of us are all focused on the human right of marriage equality, let's not forget that the fight doesn't end with same-sex marriage. We need to legalize polygamy, too. Legalized polygamy in the United States is the constitutional, feminist, and sex-positive choice. More importantly, it would actually help protect, empower, and strengthen women, children, and families. . . ."

That's just another way of calling evil "good."

As one article accurately summarizes, "The definition of marriage today has become fluid and open to debate regarding its very definition. As a result, heterosexual marriage is now no better or worse than homosexual "marriage," and marriage between two consenting adults is not inherently more or less "correct" than marriage among three (or four, or six) consenting adults. Though polygamists are a minority — a tiny minority, in fact — freedom has no value unless it extends to even the smallest and most marginalized groups among us."[2]

So a growing contingency is fighting for "marriage equality" until it extends to every same-sex couple in the United States. But they're not stopping there. The erosion of America's moral foundation clearly personifies Solomon's words,

> Where there is no prophetic vision the people cast off restraint; but blessed is he who keeps the law (Prov. 29:18).

Clarke's commentary states: "Where Divine revelation, and the faithful preaching of the sacred testimonies, are neither reverenced nor attended, the ruin of that land is at no great distance."[3]

Once a culture abandon's God's law (the absolute authority of the Word of God), then ruin is sure to follow. As America continues rejecting a worldview based on God's Word, the floodgates will be opened — and anything goes. Be warned — those activists who have been successful in opening the door to gay "marriage" across the country know this is only the start.

---

2. http://www.slate.com/articles/double_x/doublex/2013/04/legalize_polygamy_marriage_equality_for_all.html.

3. www.pinknews.co.uk/2013/01/25/comment-the-same-sex-marriage-bill-isnt-the-end-of-the-journey-towards-gay-rights/.

In an article in the UK *Pink News* entitled "The same-sex marriage bill isn't the end of the journey towards gay rights," Chris Ashford, Reader in Law and Society at the University of Sunderland argues at the end of his article:

> Legislative victory should not mean identity erasure. There remain numerous sexual freedoms to campaign on — yes sexual — that's what gay rights is about, not merely a civil rights campaign — and there are battles still to be won. Battles relating to pornography, the continued criminalization of consensual sexual acts, re-constructing our ideas of relationships in relation to sex, monogamy and the illusion that only "couples" might want to enter into a state-sanctioned partnership, are just a handful which spring to mind.

From a Christian perspective, I actually agree with him. For when people believe there are no absolute restraints, when there is no respect for God's law — *anything* goes — ruin is on the way. As went Rome, so goes the United Kingdom, Australia, and the United States of America.

Moral relativism is flooding the USA — and it's going to get much worse. The more this culture has built its worldview on man's word instead of God's Word, the more we will see our once-Christianized worldview collapsing. Increasingly, moral relativism will permeate the culture. And the more this happens, the more Christians will be seen as the enemy. Even now, Christian persecution — socially, legally — is already happening in this nation — but it's only the start!

How Firm a Foundation

Part of what makes this so tragic is that America began on such a good foundation. She had a good start. In this nation's past, there have been many reminders of a Christianized heritage in the culture, such as nativity scenes in public places, Ten Commandments displays, crosses and Christian symbols out in the open, school prayer, the teaching of creation, and even Bible reading in government schools. There was a time when abortion and gay "marriage" were illegal. All these things remind us of America's predominantly Christian roots.

But sadly, many of these foundation stones have been (and are continuing to be) removed. And with them go our national conscious and moral compass.

- 1962 — school prayer was ruled unconstitutional

- 1963 — Bible reading in school was ruled unconstitutional

- 1973 — abortion was legalized in the Roe v. Wade case

- 1985 — nativity scenes on public land were deemed to violate the so-called "separation of church and state"

- 2015 — U.S. Supreme Court legalizes gay "marriage"

Even the president himself, a man who twice placed his hand on the Word of God under oath, has publicly, enthusiastically, and unashamedly supported abortion and gay "marriage," even proclaiming June 2009 as "Lesbian, Gay, Bisexual, and Transgender Pride Month."[4]

He has also proclaimed,

> My expectation is that when you look back on these years.
> . . . You will see a time in which we as a nation finally recognize
> relationships between two men and two women as just as real
> and admirable as relationships between a man and a woman.[5]

This current president (President Obama) has indeed championed change in this nation from the Christianized worldview (and the Christian morality that once permeated the culture), to one of moral relativism.

In the past, those previously mentioned practices (Christian symbols in public places, the Bible in public schools, etc.) were reminders to the coming generations of the Christian heritage and foundation of this nation. They were also a witness to other nations concerning the true God and the truth of His Word. America was once a great Christian light in a dark world, a witness to the nations. But this has changed markedly

4. Barack Obama, "Lesbian, Gay, Bisexual, and Transgender Pride Month, 2009," The White House, http://www.gpo.gov/fdsys/pkg/FR-2009-06-04/pdf/E9-13281.pdf.

5. Barack Obama, "Remarks by the President at Human Rights Campaign Dinner," October 11, 2009, The White House, https://www.whitehouse.gov/the-press-office/remarks-president-human-rights-campaign-dinner.

in just the past few decades. That's all it took, though the seeds of change were sown many years earlier. America has become a secularized country. Moral relativism has permeated the culture. And it only takes one generation to ultimately lose a culture.

In short, this nation has changed its foundation: from God's Word to man's word. From God's unchanging ways to man's ever-changing justification for sin and immorality. We have systematically and progressively pushed God out of the picture: out of the government, out of the educational system, out of the marketplace, and even out of many churches.

And God has given us exactly what we have asked for. Like those He describes in Romans 1, we have exchanged the worship of Him to worshiping man-made religions and philosophies (like evolutionary biology, geology, astronomy, anthropology). In an ultimate sense, it is really a change of religion from God's values to man's. And as we've chosen to indulge in our own darkened desires over His ways, He has given us over to those desires and the consequences — both natural and divine — that result from them (Rom. 1:18–32).

We are fast becoming an unholy hybrid of Rome and Sodom — two cultures who rejected God and subsequently suffered His judgment. They now both lay on the figurative (and literal) ash heap of history.

This transformation has weakened us to the eventual point of collapse. But while discerning believers point out these cracks in our foundation, offering real solutions, those who promote such evil consider these changes to be "unnecessary" as they consider godliness and decency to be part of an outdated, archaic biblical moral code.

Sadly, many churches and Bible colleges/seminaries have also compromised God's Word by accepting the pagan, evolutionary religion of the age that attempts to explain life without God. The book *Already Compromised*, published in 2011, details the research conducted on such institutions. When the question, "Would you consider yourself to be a young-earth or old-earth Christian?" was asked, 78 percent of the heads of the religion departments answered "old earth."

An Internal Issue

Surprisingly, the Church has actually contributed to the undermining of biblical authority in America. In so doing, Christians have actually paved the way for the nation's change, helping (unwittingly in most cases) to build a worldview foundation that is becoming more man-centered and less Bible-centered.

Also, many in the Church and culture have been duped into thinking that the so-called "separation of church and state" issue (a perversion of what the First Amendment actually states concerning freedom of religion) means that the Bible and Christian symbols should be eliminated from the public sector, and thus bring in a neutral situation. But there is no such position as neutrality. Think about it. One is either for Christ or against Him! What has happened is that the religion of naturalism (atheism) has been imposed on the public education system (and on the culture as a whole), effectively making it a state-sponsored religion.

Therefore, the only way for the Christian reminders that have been removed to be restored is for Christians and the culture to return to the authoritative Word of God as the foundation for all thinking. After all, "Blessed is the nation whose God is the LORD" (Ps. 33:12).

This, then, is the face of relativism — or the idea that there is no absolute standard for right and wrong.

The rapidly declining moral state of America was the subject of a recent *New York Times* opinion piece.[6] In it, the author bemoaned the deplorable state of many of today's families and nationwide moral problems, writing,

> We now have multiple generations of people caught in recurring feedback loops of economic stress and family breakdown, often leading to something approaching an anarchy of the intimate life.

Titled "The Cost of Relativism," this opinion piece certainly shows what moral relativism is costing this nation. The author, David Brooks, states,

> It's increasingly clear that sympathy is not enough. It's not only money and better policy that are missing in these circles; it's norms. The health of society is primarily determined by the habits and virtues of its citizens. In many parts of America there

---

6. http://www.nytimes.com/2015/03/10/opinion/david-brooks-the-cost-of-relativism.html?_r=0.

> are no minimally agreed upon standards for what it means to be
> a father. There are no basic codes and rules woven into daily life,
> which people can absorb unconsciously and follow automatically.

Brooks hits the proverbial nail on the head by correctly stating that moral relativism has created a morally sick generation because there is no agreed upon standard to follow. And yet this is something Answers in Genesis has been warning about for years. As we continued rejecting the absolute authority of the Creator God and His Word in the culture, ruin and destruction are guaranteed to follow.

Brooks' solution to this pervasive problem is first "reintroducing . . . a moral vocabulary" and then "holding people responsible" and "holding everybody responsible." But herein lies the problem, for how will this relativistic culture ever decide on what values and morals to promote or prescribe? And who gets to decide? Our culture has, by and large, replaced God's absolute foundation for morality — His Word — with the idea that man now decides what truth, decency, and morality are. As soon as man decides truth, we're right back to "everyone did what was right in his own eyes" (Judg. 21:25) and you end up with a society like ours! We see this pattern repeated over and over in Scripture, and now we are seeing it in our own generation. And the pattern still repeats itself today. I predicted in the 1980s in my book *The Lie: Evolution* that the turn of our culture from basing its thinking on God's Word to man's ideas in the issue of origins would result in a steady loss of biblical morality and values across the nation. And unfortunately, that's exactly what has happened.

What people need to see is that moral relativism simply doesn't work. In any community or culture, there must be an unchanging standard for morality and ethics, and the only absolute standard that transcends culture, society, and generation is God's unchanging Word.

We've built a few buildings at Answers in Genesis, and any contractor will tell you that when pouring a foundation upon which a building will rest, that foundation must be solid, not shifting.

Jesus grew up in a carpenter's home. And he knew something about building things that last. What He later said concerning individuals equally applies to societies.

Everyone then who hears these words of mine and does them
will be like a wise man who built his house on the rock. And the
rain fell, and the floods came, and the winds blew and beat on
that house, but it did not fall, because it had been founded on
the rock. And everyone who hears these words of mine and does
not do them will be like a foolish man who built his house on
the sand. And the rain fell, and the floods came, and the winds
blew and beat against that house, and it fell, and great was the
fall of it (Matt. 7:24–27).

Unless we reverse course and return to the bedrock, foundational
Judeo-Christian beliefs in the Creator and His unchanging morality, we
too will fall. And the experiment that was once America will have failed,
having lasted only a few centuries. The cracks in our foundation are
openly visible, though some try to deny it. The truth is that we are rapidly crumbling and soon to collapse unless Christians take action.

Time to Return and Stand

Sadly, our culture and even much of the Church has rejected what
God's Word says about these foundational truths. This is what may have
prompted one of the wisest men who ever lived to write,

Righteousness exalts a nation, but sin is a reproach to any
people (Prov. 14:34).

While some may point out the need for common values and morality,
and accountability to these values, they do not point out the only true
solution to moral relativism and moral decline. Jesus Christ and His
gospel message are the only answer to our society's problems and tremendous moral landslide. As Christians, we must be bold and unwavering in sharing the good news of the gospel to our dying culture. Jesus
Christ is *still* the answer! However, increasingly we have generations who
don't understand the gospel and won't listen because they have been led
to believe the Book (God's Word) the gospel comes from is flawed in this
"scientific age." In many ways, the 20s generation is speaking a different
language and doesn't understand the gospel when it's communicated to
them in the same way the older generations have done. For instance,

generations ago, when someone said the word "God" in the public schools in America, most students and teachers would think of one God — the Creator God of the Bible. But when you say the word "God" in the public (government) schools today, most students and teachers will ask, "Which god?" — as there are many gods — the Muslim god, Hindu gods, the Buddhist concept of god, and so on. Unless one begins by defining the terms (such as God, sin, etc.) and giving the foundational history to understand the gospel, the coming generations don't "hear" the message!

I believe God has raised up the evangelistic ministries of Answers in Genesis, the Creation Museum, and the coming Ark Encounter in our day to call both Church and culture to return to a firm stand on the authority of the Word of God. We are here to do our part! And understanding the culture and how the coming generations think and interpret words is key to knowing how to present the gospel in this era of history. At Answers in Genesis, the Creation Museum, and Ark Encounter, we have a unique way of presenting the gospel — by starting at the beginning. This is the same way God does it in the Bible! And we define the words we use (God, sin, etc.) so those listening understand the message. We also present the answers to the skeptical questions people have today because they have been so brainwashed in evolutionary humanistic ideas. Such brainwashing (which intensely occurs in much of the public education system that most kids from the Church attend) has resulted in the coming generations doubting God's Word from the very beginning. We use creation and general Bible apologetics to deal with this doubt and unbelief, so they will listen as we explain the terms and give them the foundational history to then understand the saving gospel message.

In May 2015, news headlines appeared across America and around the world similar to this one from CNN: "America's Changing Religious Landscape," which clearly shows Christianity declining in America. Headlines appeared in secular news sources stating: "Millennials leaving church in droves, study finds."[7]

The actual survey (conducted by the Pew Research Center) stated:

---

7. http://www.cnn.com/2015/05/12/living/pew-religion-study/.

But the major new survey of more than 35,000 Americans by the Pew Research Center finds that the percentage of adults (ages 18 and older) who describe themselves as Christians has dropped by nearly eight percentage points in just seven years, from 78.4% in an equally massive Pew Research survey in 2007 to 70.6% in 2014. Over the same period, the percentage of Americans who are religiously unaffiliated — describing themselves as atheist, agnostic or "nothing in particular" — has jumped more than six points, from 16.1% to 22.8%. And the share of Americans who identify with non-Christian faiths also has inched up, rising 1.2 percentage points, from 4.7% in 2007 to 5.9% in 2014.

This just verifies the alarm Answers in Genesis has been sounding for years, and the dire need to proclaim the truth of God's Word and the gospel as we are doing at AiG, through the Creation Museum and through the life-size ark (the Ark Encounter).

As we ponder the cultural changes that seem to be escalating before our eyes, my wife often says to me:

> My heart aches as I think about the culture our grandchildren are growing up in — what are they going to be dealing with? It's so important we help train them to stand solidly on God's Word, knowing how to defend the faith. They are going to have so many pressures to deal with if the anti-Christian sentiment keeps growing as it is — I pray God will protect them and help them to be strong in their faith!

Imagine if you could open a window and look into the future to see where America will be spiritually in coming generations. What would you see?

Actually, Answers in Genesis has opened that window, in fact *two* windows — and what we see burdens us even more to ramp up the spread of God's Word and the gospel as we "contend for the faith."

> Window 1: Our 2014 research analyzing the state of the 20s (and 40s) age groups in our churches by America's Research Group (ARG).

Window 2: In the first half of 2015, we contracted with ARG to conduct a general population study to determine how many people will come to the life-size ark when it's eventually opened.

As part of that research, we asked them to also find out the spiritual state of the general population.

As we specifically consider the 20-somethings (ages 20–29), we can get a glimpse of what the "new America" will be if this culture continues on the same downward spiraling path it is on spiritually.

What a critical time it is to publicly, boldly, and unashamedly "contend for the faith" and to call both Church and culture back to the authority of the Word of God.

I've already shared some of these results, but let's consider the research in more detail, taking a look into these windows and into the future.

Window 1 — looking into the 20s age group in churches today. The 20s group (often the group called "the Millennials"), will be the leaders of the culture in the near future.

Of those in their 20s who attend church regularly:

(a) Over 40% state they are not born again.

(b) 35% state the Bible has errors or they don't know if it has errors.

(c) Close to 90% attend public school.

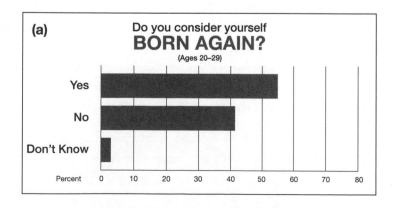

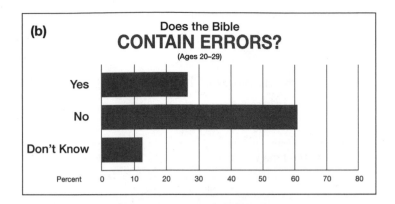

(b)

Does the Bible
CONTAIN ERRORS?
(Ages 20–29)

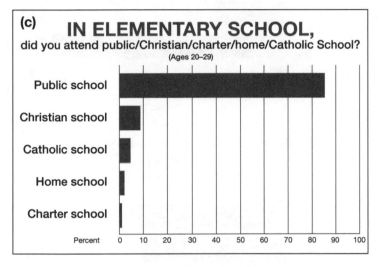

(c)
IN ELEMENTARY SCHOOL,
did you attend public/Christian/charter/home/Catholic School?
(Ages 20–29)

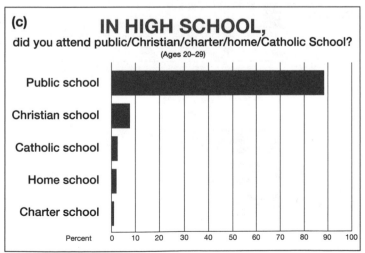

(c)
IN HIGH SCHOOL,
did you attend public/Christian/charter/home/Catholic School?
(Ages 20–29)

(d) 23% left high school believing the Bible was less true.

(e) Over 45% said they were not taught to defend their faith at Sunday school.

(f) 44% say either homosexual behavior is not a sin or they don't know if it is a sin.

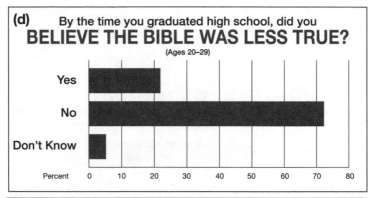

(d) By the time you graduated high school, did you
BELIEVE THE BIBLE WAS LESS TRUE?
(Ages 20–29)

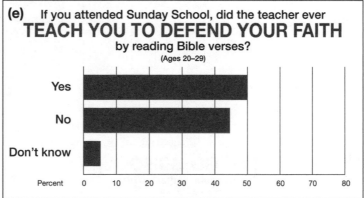

(e) If you attended Sunday School, did the teacher ever
TEACH YOU TO DEFEND YOUR FAITH
by reading Bible verses?
(Ages 20–29)

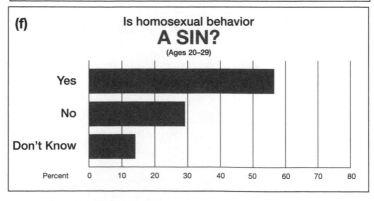

(f) Is homosexual behavior
A SIN?
(Ages 20–29)

(g) 40% believe "gay couples" should be allowed to marry and have legal rights and an additional 10% say they don't know if they should or not.

(h) 22% believe there are other books (other than the Bible) that are inspired by God and an additional 11% don't know if there are.

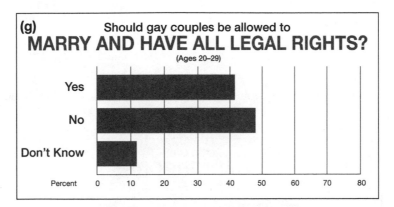

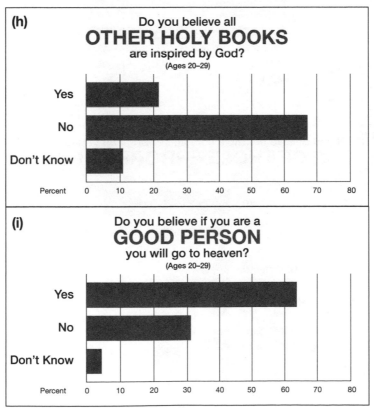

(i) 65% believe if you are a good person you will go to heaven.

Our research also showed conclusively that the issue of the age of the earth/universe was one of the major factors causing this generation to doubt the Bible can be trusted as the inerrant Word of God.

(j) 20% believe the Bible contains errors (and an additional 12% don't know if it has errors).

For those who say the Bible has errors, when asked to identify one of those errors, the age of the earth was one of the biggest issues. Also note that problems with the Book of Genesis and specifically the Flood of

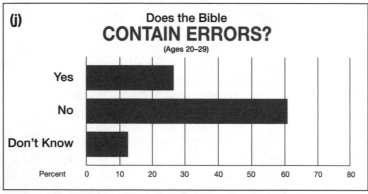

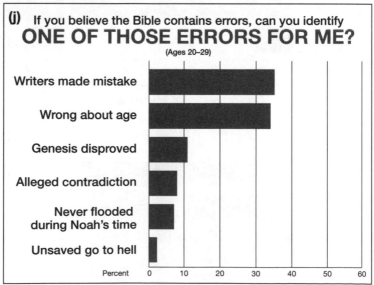

Noah's day also rated highly. In other words, the origins issue is a major issue with those who believe the Bible has errors.

When the researchers then gave the options listed in the graph and asked the question, "Which of these makes you question the Bible the most?"

(k) the majority picked the age of the earth as the major issue.

(l) 23% said someone had challenged their Christian faith.

When asked which Christian principle they were challenged on, the age of the earth was one of the biggest issues.

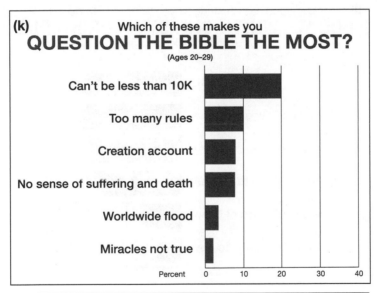

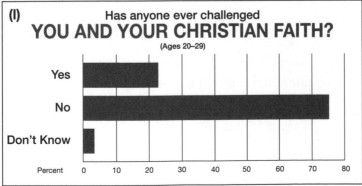

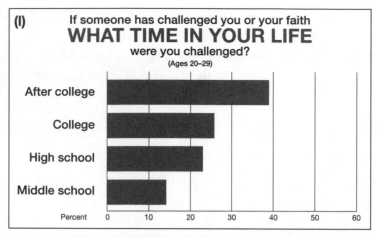

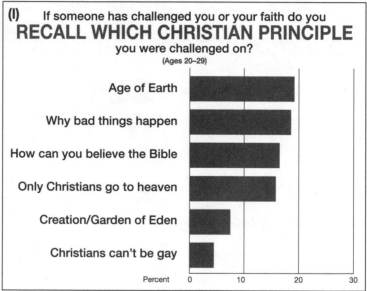

Our previous research and 40 years of ministry experience clearly shows that the majority of Christian leaders either compromise with millions of years or say the age of the earth/universe doesn't matter. Yet, our 2009 *Already Gone* published research showed the age of the earth was a significant problem among the two-thirds of the 20s age group that was leaving the church by college age. This new research confirms this is an issue. In a way it's a "big elephant" in the room in our churches that most Christian leaders either refuse to acknowledge or endorse the compromise with millions of years.

Don't you sigh when you read the above statistics? Aren't you troubled and burdened when you realize that these are the 20s group *that attend church!* There's something dreadfully wrong here.

The Reshaping of a Nation

Now let's look at Window 2.

In the general population study for the ark research, our researchers also found the following:

a. Of those who regularly attended church as children, 22% of the 60s age group had stopped attending, but 53% of the 20s age group had stopped attending.

b. 86% of the 60s age group believe Noah's ark was actually built, but only 52% of the 20s age group believe this.

c. 60% of the 60s age group believe the Christian faith is under attack today, but only 34% of the 20s group believe this.

There is much more revealing detail in the sad results of this research, but there is no doubt that the 20s group in the churches and in the world is much more secular than previous generations.

Remember, it only takes one generation to lose a culture. And we are certainly seeing the loss of the once predominantly Christianized worldview in our culture.

This generation — the 20s age group — if it doesn't change, will clearly represent a fundamentally new America.

Back in 2009, Answers in Genesis published the book *Already Gone.* This book detailed research by ARG into the 20s age group that once attended church regularly but had left the Church. Nearly two-thirds of the 20-somethings are in this group.

We found out then, and have found out again in our new 2014 research on the Church, that the acceptance of millions of years (old earth) by the majority of church leaders, the lack of teaching of apologetics in churches and Christian homes, and the effect of public school education are hands down the major reasons the 20-somethings are leaving the Church.

This 20s age group within and without the Church increasingly have a very secular worldview. And most of the ones who still attend church regularly don't really understand Christianity.

Back in 2011, I co-authored the book *Already Compromised*. In it, we dealt with research ARG conducted on the state of primarily conservative Christian universities, Bible colleges, and seminaries.

In this study, the beliefs/teachings of their presidents, vice-presidents, and heads of the science and religion (Bible) departments were researched. Sadly, as stated previously, we found that the majority of them believe in millions of years. We also found many other shocking and revealing statistics regarding the sad state of the majority of these institutions. Parents need to carefully research Christian colleges before sending their students off to an institution that could sadly undermine the foundation of their Christian faith.

So that's the bad news! In reality, it's much worse than the summary I've given you above, as there were so many other areas that show that so many of the 20s group in the Church do not have a Christian worldview.

You may wonder, "But what can we do? It seems so overwhelming." Many have said to me they just get depressed and feel like giving up and waiting for Jesus to come.

But we need to listen to how God's Word instructs us. In Luke 19 we read a parable by Jesus:

> A nobleman went into a far country to receive for himself a kingdom and then return. Calling ten of his servants, he gave them ten minas, and said to them, *"Engage in business until I come"* (Luke 19:12–14, emphasis added).

One translation states, "occupy till I come."

Jesus gives Christians (His servants), talents and gifts that they are to use until He comes. The point is, we need to be faithful in being about the Master's work — *regardless* of what we see happening around us. We don't know where we are in the time-line of the last days — if anything, we need to be more fired up, more passionate, show more "righteous anger" (like Nehemiah), and be more urgent in proclaiming the truth of God's Word and the gospel so people will hear and listen.

Too Late for a U-Turn?

Perhaps you've heard the fictional account of radio transmission between American and Canadian authorities off the coast of Newfoundland during a heavy fog. This radio conversation reads,

U.S. Naval Vessel: "Please divert your course 15 degrees to the north to avoid a collision."

Canadians: "Negative. Recommend you divert YOUR course 15 degrees to the South to avoid a collision."

U.S. Naval Vessel: "This is the captain of a U.S. Navy ship. I say again, divert YOUR course."

Canadians: "No, I say again, you divert YOUR course."

U.S. Naval Vessel: "THIS IS THE AIRCRAFT CAR-RIER *USS ABRAHAM LINCOLN*, THE SECOND LARG-EST SHIP IN THE UNITED STATES' ATLANTIC FLEET. WE ARE ACCOMPANIED BY THREE DESTROYERS, THREE CRUISERS, AND NUMEROUS SUPPORT VES-SELS. I DEMAND THAT YOU CHANGE YOUR COURSE 15 DEGREES NORTH. THAT'S ONE-FIVE DEGREES NORTH, OR COUNTER MEASURES WILL BE UNDER-TAKEN TO ENSURE THE SAFETY OF THIS SHIP."

Canadians: "This is a lighthouse. Your call."

While humorous, this apocryphal story nonetheless illustrates a sobering truth. We are a country very much like that ship's captain — blind, misguided, trusting his instincts instead of the facts, and way too stubborn to admit he is wrong. What we need is national course correction that begins with repentance. Though originally made in the context of God's relationship to His covenant people, Israel, the principle of repentance and blessing applies to us today as well.

If my people who are called by my name humble themselves, and pray and seek my face and turn from their wicked ways, then I will hear from heaven and will forgive their sin and heal their land (2 Chron. 7:14).

Notice God's word to King Solomon begins with a call to humility. If we are to ever turn back the tide of relativism, we must first humble ourselves before God. This means admitting that man and his foolish ideas and ways have failed. So can we do this? Is it possible? Can we bow our stiff necks before Almighty God, or will we continue in the charade of pretending we know better than Him?

Humility, however, is only the beginning. God also requires that we pray, seek His face, and turn from our wicked ways. We have to repent of the cancerous evils we've allowed to plague our nation. Homosexuality, gay "marriage," abortion, and the pagan religion of evolutionary thought — those are the altars we've built to the gods of pluralism, relativism, atheism, and immorality. And like ancient Israel, we must tear down those altars and return to the godly values and pursuits that once made this country great. It is *only then* that God will hear from heaven, forgive our sin, and heal our land.

However, this healing will not magically happen on its own. We cannot continue depending on political leaders to right the wrongs in our country. Rather, it's the Holy Spirit, working through you and the Church that must be the initial and primary catalyst causing such radical, sweeping change. According to 2 Thessalonians 2:6–7, God's Spirit working in the Church is the current restraining influence in the world today preventing evil from completely flooding our land. And though there is no promised last days' revival in Scripture prior to the Rapture, that doesn't mean there will not be one. Even so, if we are to begin turning things around in the right direction, we must be willfully intentional and spiritually strategic. And such a "turning things around" must begin in the home and church!

No White Flag

There is no doubt that we are in a war. It's a cultural conflict and a moral battle. It's a fight for the minds of a generation. Our ultimate enemy is not people, but rather an entity whose mission is to destroy those whom God loves. Paul wrote to the Ephesian believers,

> For we do not wrestle against flesh and blood, but against the rulers, against the authorities, against the cosmic powers

over this present darkness, against the spiritual forces of evil in the heavenly places. Therefore take up the whole armor of God, that you may be able to withstand in the evil day, and having done all, to stand firm (Eph. 6:12–13).

Our adversary, the devil, roams about like a roaring lion, seeking someone to devour (1 Pet. 5:8). And though these words are directed at believers, Satan also seeks to destroy humanity itself. Like a thief, he comes only to "steal and kill and destroy" (John 10:10). His greatest desire is to blind people to the gospel and keep them from experiencing the forgiveness, freedom, and salvation found in Jesus Christ (2 Cor. 4:4).

Because we have such a formidable enemy, this is precisely why believers must be educated, trained, equipped, and armed with the will to do battle, even if it comes down to the last man.

This courageous spirit is modeled throughout the Bible, and is what separated men and women of faith from the vast compromising crowd. It's a ferocious faith that refuses to give up.

We see it in Moses, leading two million Hebrews out of Egypt and across the Red Sea in the midst of impossible odds.

We see it in Joshua, taking the next generation of Jews into the conquest of the Promised Land, and just before his death, challenging an entire nation, "Choose this day whom you will serve, whether the gods your fathers served in the region beyond the River, or the gods of the Amorites in whose land you dwell. But as for me and my house, we will serve the LORD" (Josh. 24:15).

We see it in young David, who refused to stand by and let a pagan giant taunt the armies of the living God.

We see it in Paul who could not tolerate seeing so many idols in Athens. Something moved him to speak. Paul wasn't merely "street preaching." He was engaging his culture by reaching them where they were and demonstrating the evidence for the true God (Acts 17).

We see it on display through the lives of faith's heroes in Hebrews 11 — men and women who fought valiantly in the fields of faith, casting aside comfort for something better that awaited them.

But nowhere do we see this spirit of courage, faith, and perseverance displayed more than with the Lord Jesus Christ. If ever there was a time to give up the fight, it was when He was arrested in the Garden of Geth-semane. If ever there was a time to turn back, it was when He was being whipped and beaten beyond belief. If ever there was a time to surrender and raise a white flag, it was at the Cross when God the Father unleashed the full fury of eternal wrath on Him.

And yet He persevered. But why?

Hebrews 12:1–2 tells us why:

> Therefore, since we are surrounded by so great a cloud of witnesses, let us also lay aside every weight, and sin which clings so closely, and let us run with endurance the race that is set before us, looking to Jesus, the founder and perfecter of our faith, *who for the joy that was set before him endured the cross, despising the shame*, and is seated at the right hand of the throne of God (emphasis added).

Jesus, the fountainhead of faith itself, is the One who perfectly mod-eled it for us. He endured the horror of the Cross, disregarding the shame associated with such a death because of the "*joy* that was set before Him." But what kind of joy is this referring to? I believe there are three possibilities:

1. The joy of having pleased His Father, and to have fulfilled the mission/work God sent Him to do (John 17:4)

2. The joy of being reinstated at the right hand of the Father fol-lowing His Resurrection (John 17:5; Heb. 1:3, 12:2)

3. The joy of accomplishing salvation for sinners like you and me (Heb. 2:10)

Perhaps His joy encompassed all three of these honorable goals, seeing as how they were all realized once the suffering of the Cross had run its course.

It is His enduring faith, forged through a life of obedience and tested through suffering that we seek to emulate. And it is exactly His example we look to when encountering opposition in our walk of faith. So many Christians cringe at the slightest sign of hostility, challenge, or backlash regarding their beliefs. But the author of Hebrews reminds us that we have not "resisted to the point of shedding . . . blood" like our Lord did (Heb. 12:4). And even then, He did not surrender the fight. His example is the reason we "may not grow weary or fainthearted" (Heb. 12:3).

Jesus fought and endured to the end because He had a passion to honor the Father. He fought because He longed to return to His rightful place of authority at the Father's side. And He persevered because He knew there was something worth fighting for.

You.

You and I are alive in God today because He stayed the course. Jesus did not allow the Pharisees and religious teachers of His day to misinterpret and compromise the Word of God. He corrected them, showing God's people a better way (Matt. 5–7, 23).

When Christ ascended back to heaven following His Resurrection, He left His disciples in charge of carrying on the task of "making disciples" (Matt. 28:18–20). Deputizing them with the power of the Holy Spirit (Acts 1:8), they were to take His life changing gospel to the nations, even to the "uttermost part of the earth" (KJV). Anything that undermines that message by subverting the truth of God's Word must be fought. Our war is not waged out of hatred *against* people, but rather due to love *for* them. It is a war to redeem, rescue, and deliver them from lies which blind them to the truth and saving grace of Jesus Christ.

There is a time for tolerance, a time to turn the other cheek, and a time to be silent. But there is also a time to fight. But it's not just fighting for fighting's sake. Or even just to be "right" or win an argument. It's doing battle for the sake of humanity, the Christian faith, and the glory of God. Unlike other religions that wage "holy wars," spilling the blood of their enemies and the innocent, being a "soldier of the cross" means fighting on your knees before moving forward into the workplace, the marketplace, the high school and university classroom. But as we've seen, the battle must also be fought in our own churches. We must lovingly challenge our church's leadership to go before us into battle through equipping an army of Christ-followers.

The best way to change a society or culture is not to enact laws but to redeem hearts. After all, God's Word teaches us, "For as he thinketh in his heart, so is he"(Prov. 23:7; KJV). It seems the secularists understand this principle more than many Christians! Secularists have captured the minds of generations of kids from the Church, and now they are capturing their hearts also. In many ways, so many Christians handed their children over to the secularists (such as in the public education system) to be trained, and now we wonder why we are losing them from the Church. And we wonder why even many of those young people in the Church have such a secularized worldview! Christians need to be active in training their children as the Bible instructs us — from birth.

And what happens should we remain mediocre and silent, hiding behind the walls of our homes and churches? Should this be our strategy, we as a nation will certainly become Rome. It is foolish naiveté and ignorance to think otherwise. We will become Sodom and Gomorrah. And the floodwaters of evil will continue to rise, drowning out the voice of righteousness.

As Christians though, we do not quit. The word "surrender" is not in our vocabulary. We do not give up. It is not in our spiritual DNA, as we are by nature overcomers. "Greater is he that is in you, than he that is in the world" (1 John 4:4; KJV). Among the most admirable characteristics followers of Christ possess is the ability to persevere.

So take down your white flag of surrender. Burn it if you need to. And in its place raise the banner of the Cross. Lift high the standard of truth in your heart, home, and church. Let the light of God's truth in your words and deeds shine before all men, so that they may see and glorify your Father who is in heaven.

Chapter 9

A Game Plan

Start at Home

So where do we go from here? How should these truths we've discussed impact us going forward? What should be our strategy and what are some practical ways to implement it?

To begin with, it's no secret that there is a crisis of leadership today in the Christian home. And unfortunately, men are often the most difficult group to motivate toward spirituality. You could attempt to blame this on the pressure and preoccupation men have with making a living and providing for their families. But Scripture tells a different story. This spiritual passivity in Christian men traces its roots all the way back to Genesis, to the very beginning of mankind itself.

In Genesis 2 we see God creating Adam, giving him responsibility to cultivate and keep the garden He's provided (Gen. 2:15). God then created woman from Adam's rib, appointing him as head, leader, and protector over her (Gen. 2:21–23; Eph. 5:22–27). But when we read the account of the serpent's temptation in Genesis 3, we find the man strangely absent in his leadership role. Instead of protecting and shielding his wife from the serpent's influence, he stood idly by while she was tempted into sin. Though not explicitly mentioned, when Eve gave the fruit to her husband in Genesis 3:6, it is assumed that he was nearby. Following God's declaration that it was "not good that the man should be alone" (Gen. 2:18), and Adam, having felt the void of not having a "helper suitable" for him in 2:20, it makes sense that the man and woman were virtually inseparable as newlyweds. The "cleaving" (bonding commitment) of the man to the woman goes far beyond a mere sexual purpose, but extends to the emotional, relational, and spiritual aspects of their union. They were *together*.

Thus, Adam exhibited passivity in his leadership when he allowed his wife to be deceived by the devil. Today, we see man's sin demonstrated either in blatant passivity or in dominating his wife, "lording" his influence over her. Both are unscriptural. Further, as part of the post-sin curse upon humanity, Eve would capitalize on the man's failure to lead, and desire to "rule" over her husband (Gen. 3:16). We see this today in Christian homes where the wife is the primary spiritual influence in the children's lives. Of course she should be a powerful presence spiritually in her children's lives, but when husbands and fathers fail to initiate that leadership and influence, a void is created, and women typically fill it.

However, this is not God's design.

We need to be diligent and realize that every child conceived in a mother's womb is a being who will live forever either in heaven or hell. What a reminder of the awesome responsibility parents have to do their best to teach their children to worship the Son and to put their faith in the Lord Jesus Christ as their Creator Redeemer.

According to Scripture, the home, above everywhere else, is the epicenter of spiritual development. As God commanded Moses,

> You shall love the LORD your God with all your heart and with all your soul and with all your might. And these words that I command you today shall be on your heart. You shall *teach* them diligently to your children, and shall *talk* of them when you sit in your house, and when you *walk* by the way, and when you lie down, and when you rise. You shall bind them as a sign on your hand, and they shall be as frontlets between your eyes. You shall write them on the doorposts of your house and on your gates (Deut. 6:5–9, emphasis added).

Moses' words speak to the practical, daily nature of imparting faith to our children. It begins by loving "the Lord your God with all your heart." A dynamic relationship with God is a dad's greatest asset. It is from this vertical relationship that wisdom, patience, and endurance flows horizontally to the family. And these are three indispensable qualities in parenting. Further, having God's Word "on the heart" of the father makes it an inward reality and not just an outward expression. Though as parents we have in inherent authority over our children, our *position* as fathers is not enough to effectively raise children. Mere external pressure from parent to child may curb some behavior, but it cannot make a disciple. Our authority as parents is enhanced by our spirituality, and that begins in the heart, from the inside out. Fathers must be changed supernaturally by being born again from above. But it doesn't stop there. An effective Christian father is one who continues to progress in his faith. And nowhere is this more important than in his interaction with God's Word. Hearing from God on a regular basis is what keeps a dad strong, centered, and tethered to the anchor of faith. This spiritual transformation is essential to male leadership in the home.

Next, Moses outlines practical ways to impart wisdom and faith to our children, using three memorable words.

Teach — "You shall teach them diligently to your children." This speaks of a commitment to faithfulness on the part of fathers to consistently communicate God's character and truth to their children. Remember the account of Mary and Martha of Bethany? Dr. Luke writes of one particular scene in chapter 10, verses 38–42 of his gospel. Martha is busy serving the Lord, preparing a meal for Him. A worthy task? Yes. An honorable offering? Absolutely. But meanwhile, Mary is "doing nothing," just sitting at the feet of Jesus, soaking in His words. So Martha tells Jesus to rebuke Mary for not serving. Jesus responds by politely but firmly telling Martha to back off, because Mary had chosen a higher and more important activity. Mary would later serve Jesus in a way the whole world would remember (John 12:1–8; Mark 14:3–9). Martha could have taken some lessons on spirituality from her sister.

So Jesus also elevated the importance of teaching the Word of God in His ministry. For us to do this in the home, I believe we must be diligent to communicate the Scriptures in a way that is both accurate and relevant. And this includes teaching them to defend the Christian faith against the attacks of our day.

Again, Jesus is our model, as He spent times of *formal teaching* with His disciples (Matt. 5:1–2). These are the "official" times set aside to impart truth to our children, both at home and when the church gathers. These times are planned and scheduled. They take place at prearranged times and often require some advance preparation.

The second word Moses uses to describe imparting the faith in the home is *talk*. — This refers to the informal discussions about God, His Word, life, and spirituality. It naturally happens when you "sit in the house," or times when your family is together. It doesn't mean every conversation has to be a spiritual one, but just that your home has a "godly ambience" about it. It means talking about the Lord is a natural thing for your family, and not something that's forced or awkward.

The third way Moses counsels us to lead our family spiritually is to *walk* — ". . . when you *walk* by the way, and when you lie down, and when you rise." This type of communication is *spontaneous* and unplanned. Jesus would use these "life moments" to teach spiritual truth to his disciples (Mark 8:14–21). Someone has wisely noted that truth is more often "caught" than "taught." And certainly the Master Teacher demonstrated this truth as He regularly took advantage of "teachable moments" to impart knowledge and wisdom from God. It's a way for a family leader to look for God in life, and pass that knowledge and wisdom on to his kids.

Moses concludes by commanding Israel to "bind them [God's words] as a sign on your hand, and they shall be as frontlets between your eyes. You shall write them on the doorposts of your house and on your gates." Though the Jews literally did this, the idea here is that your home and family are permeated with truth from Scripture. Again, it's a heart issue. A Scripture verse written on a plaque in a home is simply decoration unless it is also written on the hearts of those who live in that home.

While we cannot downplay the role of a wife and mother in spiritual influence and "training up a child," the initial and primary responsibility lies with the man. Like Adam in the Garden, he is ultimately responsible for the spiritual well-being of his wife and children, and he will answer to God for that stewardship (Gen. 3:9).

The Role of the Local Church

A second critical area of influence is, of course, in the church. America is joining the trend among Western nations to slide into secularism and unbelief. This downward spiral has impacted churches and Christian homes, as well. Two-thirds of children will leave the Church after they leave home, and very few return. So what's missing in their lives? What can we do to stop the exodus and these times of great difficulty in the Church?

Through what Paul called a "falling away from the faith," many churches and even denominations have abandoned the faith Jesus commanded them to pass on (1 Tim. 4:1). I believe this is part of the "times of difficulty" the Apostle spoke of in 2 Timothy 3:1–5:

> But understand this, that in the last days there will come times of difficulty. For people will be lovers of self, lovers of money, proud, arrogant, abusive, disobedient to their parents, ungrateful, unholy, heartless, unappeasable, slanderous, without self-control, brutal, not loving good, treacherous, reckless, swollen with conceit, lovers of pleasure rather than lovers of God, having the appearance of godliness, but denying its power. Avoid such people.

And what was Paul's remedy for this coming epidemic of apostasy? "Stay true to the Word of God!" (2 Tim. 3:14–17).

Two words stand out in Paul's admonition to pastor Timothy. The first is "learned." Timothy had been taught the Scripture "from childhood," faithfully passed down to him from his grandmother to his mother, and then finally to Timothy (2 Tim. 2:1–5). That's *three generations of faith*, preserved and passed down. And now Timothy was doing the same thing with "faithful men," who in turn were to "teach others also." It was important for Paul that Timothy "continue" in the truths he had learned and come to embrace by faith. Many churches today are focused on using their church services and ministries for evangelistic purposes, often to the neglect of equipping believers.

But the primary job of the organized church is to train followers of Christ, *not* reach the world (Eph. 4:11ff). Believers themselves are to be salt and light, reaching the lost with the gospel as they go into the world (Matt. 28:18–20). We have reversed this mandate, removing the stewardship of the individual Christian for evangelism and instead abdicating it to the corporate church. But the church's job is "to equip the saints for the work of ministry, for building up of the body of Christ" (Eph. 4:12). We gather for edification and equipping and scatter into the world for evangelism. But when "doing church" for the purpose of attracting the unsaved is what drives Sunday morning services, the church has lost her way.

This kind of Pauline "discipleship learning" is part of what's missing in Christian churches and homes today. We have the appearance of godliness (what Paul refers to as a "form of godliness" in 2 Tim. 3:5), but the supernatural power of this godliness is being denied because of a preoccupation with pleasing and entertaining self (2 Tim. 3:1–4). In a church culture obsessed with consumerism and "customer satisfaction," there is little room to think of others or giving your life away for the sake of another, perhaps younger, disciple. Many churches focus their energy on elaborate Sunday morning productions to attract people — instead of emphasizing the teaching of the Word and equipping God's people to answer the skeptical questions of our day. There is nothing wrong with music, drama, or technology, of course, but I'm talking about the main emphasis within the church. Sadly, many churches think entertainment is what the 20s generation wants, instead of giving them the answers they need to know so they can trust God's Word from the beginning. Personally, I've found the 20s generation to be hungry for answers! But the Church also needs to be involved in training men to be husbands and fathers, and women to be wives and mothers.

It has been wisely stated, "You cannot impart what you do not possess." If you haven't been taught, trained, discipled, and equipped, there's no chance you will do the same things for someone else.

Consequently, most fathers haven't been taught to be the spiritual head by their church. Nevertheless, part of the church's role should be to teach and help fathers to be the spiritual heads of their homes. And how is this to be done? Why not do it like Jesus and Paul did? Find faithful men who are hungry to be the men God wants them to be and "entrust" the truth of God to them. In the Church, we often obsess over planning, packaging, programming, and ministries. For Jesus and Paul, what mattered was spending time with men in order to invest the Word into them. What that looks like in a particular church is not as important as the fact that it gets done. We cannot let *form* trump *substance*. Every church should be committed to discipling men. And this training and equipping must be *comprehensive*. Remember, Jesus had a relatively short amount of time to impart a very large amount of truth to His disciples, and yet He had resolved in His heart to give them a wide variety of content. But it wasn't just content for content's sake. Jesus gave His closest followers a well-rounded theological education. He wanted their knowledge of God to be comprehensive, and that necessitated much time teaching them. In John 17:4–8, Jesus gives us a private look into His innermost thoughts and feelings as He prays His great high priestly prayer. In it, He tells the Father He has completed the work He was given to do (4), having faithfully "manifested your name to the people whom you gave me out of the world" (6). This took place, Jesus prays, because he had given them "the words that you gave me," and they accepted them (8).

Paul followed Jesus' example, motivating him to declare the "whole counsel of God" to the believers at Ephesus during his three-year stay there. (Acts 20:27–31).

What this says to us is that pastors should teach the whole Bible to the church. Not that they have to cover every detail in Scripture's 66 books, but the idea is that they are given a solid working understanding of the Bible as a whole, along with an ability to understand and articulate a defense of God's Word and the person and work of Christ. This helps to ensure churches produce a generation of well-rounded and fully equipped disciples.

Specifically, this means teaching through books of the Bible, overviews of Scripture, Bible study books, Bible-based Christian books, topical studies, the attributes of God, the fundamentals of the faith, basic Christian doctrines, character studies and modern-day issues and how Scripture speaks to them, and in-depth general Bible and creation apologetics. At times of national crisis or newsworthy items regarding theology or morality, it is necessary to "capture the moment" by taking a break from what you're studying to address or discuss a certain issue (e.g., school shootings, war, moral issues, terrorism, attack on the family, death and suffering and a loving God, etc.). Doing this mirrors in the Church what Moses commanded Israel to do in the home — demonstrating that Scripture is "living and active" and applies to any and all life situations.

I am reminded of 1 Chronicles 12:32 and the sons of Issachar, "who had understanding of the times. . . ." These men interpreted the times in which they lived and applied wisdom regarding what needed to be done. Christian parents today need to understand the times we live in and what needs to be taught to their children — how to pass the spiritual legacy on to the coming generations and influence the world for Christ.

No one would ever say that "training up a child" was an easy task. It involves time, energy, preparation, and hard work over much time. It requires the Church and family to cooperate and work together for the common good of our young people and for the greater glory of our God.

It's all about *investment*, which is the heart of discipleship. It's what Jesus did, what Paul practiced, and what got the Church this far in history. Though challenging and often risky, I firmly believe it pays off and comes back to bless you in the long run.

Additionally, the ripple effects of this discipleship from pastor to congregation extends beyond the home to the community as well. As Christians, we need bold, brave, and equipped brothers and sisters who will become active in their communities, school boards, and other organizations in order to promote godly change from the bottom up. Isn't that what being "salt and light" is all about? In these settings, Christians can ask challenging questions about the exclusion of sound Christian values from schools, the acceptance of the religion of humanism, and the absence of critical thinking when it comes to teaching evolution, etc. Based on the U.S. Constitution, no single religion should be endorsed in a government-run school. Unless we stand up to challenge these ideas, the schools will continue to indoctrinate students with the religious beliefs of humanists.[1] At the present time, the government in America is using tax dollars to fund indoctrinating students in public schools in a religion — the religion of naturalism (which is atheism).

The first step is for dads and moms (God's leaders in the home) to take this cultural and spiritual crisis seriously and then to become equipped in defending their faith. Talk to your pastor. Mobilize and organize a group of parents, other adults, and teenagers for a series in basic apologetics. Contact us at AiG and we can connect you to the appropriate resources. If Christian parents truly understood the intensity of the warfare in which we are engaged, they would not hesitate to pursue such a course of action.

The time is now!

Public School, Private Decision

In the last chapter, I stated that an "elephant in the room" was the fact that so many Christian leaders have compromised with millions of years or ignore this issue that our research has shown has had a significant influence on the 20s generation in regard to doubting and disbelieving Scripture.

But there's another "elephant in the room" that also needs to be dealt with. It's one many parents and Christian leaders won't address, or don't know how to, or don't have the courage to. But we need to face it head on!

Nearly 90 percent of kids from church homes attend public (government) schools in America. Now consider all that's been shown about the state of the 20s generation in the Church — and in the culture as a

---

1. Answers in Genesis is often misrepresented as trying to get creationist teaching into the public schools. AiG does not lobby any government agencies to include the teaching of biblical creation in the public schools. We do not believe that teaching biblical creation should be mandated in public school science classrooms. If it were mandated, it would likely be taught poorly (and possibly mockingly) by a teacher who does not understand what the Bible teaches and who believes in evolution. At the same time, it is not right that the tenets of secular humanism can be taught at the exclusion of Christian ideas. This type of exclusivity does not promote the critical thinking skills of students demanded by most science education standards. Teachers should be allowed, at the very least, the academic freedom to present various models of the history of life on earth and teach the strengths and weaknesses of those models. Recognizing that in the current political climate we can only expect to see evolution taught, it is only reasonable to include teaching the shortcomings of evolutionary ideas.

whole. I will go on record as stating that public education has had a devastating effect on children — including those from church homes. Most students do not ultimately survive the public school system spiritually, and those that do have been negatively influenced in many ways that most don't realize.

We have many of the science textbooks used in public schools in America in our library at Answers in Genesis. Over and over again these textbooks teach students that science does not involve the supernatural, and science can only allow explanations involving natural processes. Naturalism is nothing but atheism! Most public schools have, by and large, thrown out God, the Bible, prayer, and creation teaching. They now claim they are neutral, and not religious. But that is simply not true. Now such schools are imposing the religion of naturalism or atheism on generations of students.

From a biblical perspective, we are taught, "He who is not with Me is against Me; and he who does not gather with Me scatters" (Matt. 12:30; NASB). There is no neutral position here. Many Christians even think that public education is neutral in regard to religion, but this is simply not true. If the system is not for Christ, then it is against Him. If the textbooks do not harmonize with God's truth, they will naturally teach the opposite of that truth.

Do you think it would make a difference in how we view our children's training, how much time we've spent with them, who we entrust their education to if we were prepared to say, "Well, Johnny, it's Monday. I'm sending you to the church of atheism today for six hours. And then I will send you to the church of atheism for four more days this week. I do hope the hour you spend at church on Sunday will counter any wrong things you are taught."

Now I realize this is a very emotional topic for people. Many pastors know if they were to speak against the public education system, they would receive negative reactions from many, especially those who teach in government schools. But I ask you to consider this topic from a biblical perspective. How should parents view public schools?

I often hear Christian parents say something like this: "Your kids should be in the public school to witness to the other kids; you need to throw your children out into the world so they will learn to survive; they need to be mixing with non-Christian kids so they can be an example to them," and many other similar arguments. But when asked for biblical references for such a position, I often get an answer that goes something like this: "The Bible says we are to be the salt of the earth. Our children therefore need to be in the public schools so they can be salt and light to the other students." Now, it is true that Matthew 5:13 says, "You are the salt of the earth," but let's look at this passage in full context:

> *You are the salt of the earth. But if the salt loses its saltiness, how can it be made salty again? It is no longer good for anything, except to be thrown out and trampled underfoot* (NIV, emphasis added).

Mark 9:50 states something else about salt that is very important and must be taken into consideration:

> Salt is good, but if it loses its saltiness, how can you make it salty again? *Have salt among yourselves*, and be at peace with each other (NIV, emphasis added).

The point is this: *A person can't be the salt of the earth until they have salt, and it needs to be uncontaminated salt that retains its saltiness.*

Let's face it: Children are being contaminated as a result of their secular education, television, the books they read, and their friends. In a world of no absolutes, evolution, sex outside marriage, gay "marriage," attacks on gender distinction, humanism, and false religions — children will be tossed to and fro. How do they know which way to go? How do they know what to choose? They *don't*, unless they've been trained in truth and can recognize the difference between good and evil in the world. I do feel very strongly that this training is best done in the sanctifying environment of a home-based education, or diligent training at home in conjunction with a Christian school that does not compromise the Word of God, beginning in Genesis. Sadly, I have concluded from 40 years of experience in active ministry that the majority of Christian schools do compromise God's Word and really just add God to a secular worldview.

Because so many children from church homes have been trained by the government education system (which has become more and more anti-Christian over the years — to the point of eliminating Christianity totally), and because most fathers haven't really trained their children with a biblical foundation as they should, there are now generations of adults who attend church, but are so contaminated by the world that they think like the world — as we have seen in our latest research project. They lack salt, and the salt they have has lost its saltiness by contamination. These people then contaminate those around them and their own children. These children are often given no salt at all, or the little they have becomes even more contaminated than the parents' salt.

I believe that in many instances (not all, of course), what people call "teenage rebellious years" is due to a lack of being trained to acquire a taste for the things of the Lord in the early years. Once children become teenagers (and we all know that there are hormonal changes and certain behavior patterns related to puberty and adolescence), it is very difficult to change their behavior.

Contamination comes in many forms, but perhaps the saddest aspect is that much of institutional Christianity has compromised the Word of God, particularly concerning the doctrine of creation. Genesis (especially the first 11 chapters) is foundational to all Christian doctrine. Let me state my warning again: if generations are trained to disbelieve the Book of Genesis as literal history, and to embrace man's fallible ideas concerning evolution and an earth that is millions of years old, they are put on a slippery slide of unbelief through the rest of the Bible. If the Bible's *history* is not accurate, then why should the Bible's *morality* be accepted? After all, the morality is based in the history.

The literal understanding of the events in the Book of Genesis is necessary to an understanding of what Christian doctrine is all about. Sadly, some children from Christian homes are being contaminated by what are called "Christian" schools. More and more schools are being established on secular humanism and a secular curriculum to which God is added, but you can't Christianize a secular philosophy! You can't have both!

If you are going to opt for a private Christian education for your kids, don't assume *anything* when it comes to the content of the courses or the convictions of the faculty. Don't assume that the students there are going to be a positive influence on your children. Do your research on the school; monitor everything carefully, and never *shirk* your responsibility to be the one who trains your kid.

No matter what education you choose, know that you must be pouring the "salt" into your children — and this salt should be as uncontaminated as possible. Children need to be taught to acquire a taste for biblical teaching as early and as repeatedly as possible.

This process is most assured in a home-based education where the parents can take hour-by-hour responsibility for the task. A private Christian education can also be a good option, as long as a parent doesn't forget their responsibility to monitor the environment and content of the education.

Yes, we are all called to be "salt" to the world. Our children are to be this as well, but they must first be filled with pure salt from God's Word — leading to spiritual maturity and stability, so that they can be missionaries to the world without being contaminated themselves and made useless for the gospel.

Some Christian parents justify their choice of public education by saying, "Yes, but I've got *good* kids." Many child psychologists teach that children are basically "good" too, but the Bible teaches otherwise. Psalm 51:5 states, "Surely I was sinful at birth, sinful from the time my mother conceived me" (NIV). Scripture tells us that children are a precious "heritage from the LORD" (Ps. 127:3; NIV), and that they are a great blessing in a Christian home. Nevertheless, children, like adults, must be viewed first of all as sinful creatures, "For all have sinned and fall short of the glory of God" (Rom. 3:23).

I remember visiting the hospital in Australia where my sister had just had a baby. I looked at this beautiful infant and said, "What a beautiful looking sinful creature you have there!" (I was thinking of Jeremiah 17:9 that says, "The heart is deceitful above all things, and desperately sick; who can understand it?" I was nearly thrown out of the hospital, as you might imagine, but when they took this baby home, it didn't take the parents long to find out I was right!

Because of the sin nature inherent in all mankind, and the natural desires of our flesh to do evil, none of us should ever think that we are "good" enough to be able to resist temptation.

When placed in a compromising situation, we are more likely to be influenced by the bad than by the good. It's a challenge to get children to do what is right, but it is easy to let children do that which is wrong — just leave them to themselves, and they will express their true sinful tendencies.

Maturity comes with training, discipline, renewing the mind according to Scripture, and learning to walk in the power of the Holy Spirit rather than in the power of the flesh. That doesn't come naturally! It comes with maturity, and maturity takes time. Children are not miniature adults. They are unable to discriminate between good and evil. They don't have the discipline to choose between the truth and the cleverly crafted evolutionary philosophies.

Ephesians 4:14 states,

> Then we will no longer be infants, tossed back and forth by the waves, and blown here and there by every wind of teaching and by the cunning and craftiness of people in their deceitful scheming (NIV).

Paul also says in 1 Corinthians 13:11,

> When I was a child, I talked like a child, I thought like a child, I reasoned like a child. When I became a man, I put the ways of childhood behind me (NIV).

The Bible makes it clear that children are easily led astray, easily tossed to and fro, easily deceived, and so on. Because of the sin nature and the flesh, a child in a pagan environment is likely to lose saltiness faster that gaining it, even if the parent is trying hard to fill the child with uncontaminated salt at home. (Consider how much time your children spend being trained in the pagan secular system compared to how much time they receive authoritative biblical input!)

When the child becomes a man or woman, exhibiting spiritual discernment and biblical maturity, then they can maintain their salt and be salt and light to the world. Let's face it, when we as adults are given choices, our sinful tendencies draw us in the wrong direction. Would you rather read the Bible or a secular magazine? Are you more inclined to spend time praying or watching television? Would you rather go to a missions program at church or a football game at the stadium? If you have some extra money, would you prefer to buy Christian books or a new piece of furniture or new car?

I'm sure we all get the point. It's not that we shouldn't read magazines or buy a new car, but we need to consider our priorities according to what the Bible says is important, and children who still have much maturing in the Christian faith are very unlikely to do this.

So, in a sense, what I'm saying is that the salt is more likely to pour out of the children rather than to be retained by them. And if we've allowed a lot of contamination to fill up these "vessels," it is going to be very hard to "decontaminate" them. That's why parents need to work so hard to avoid as much contamination as possible, and that's why dads and moms have to work with much prayer, patience, and perseverance to ensure as much salt as possible stays in the "vessel." There also needs to be much remedial work that reminds children over and over again of biblical truths that continually instill in them a Christian worldview (and the more that happens, the more the culture as a whole will be influenced for good). And as I've stated so many times, we need to be teaching children to defend the Christian faith. An emphasis on creation apologetics and general Bible apologetics is so needed today — and it's so absent from most Christian homes and churches.

But these things are very difficult to do when the child is spending all day in an anti-God, Bible-denying, secular humanist enforcing environment.

Because of the fallen world we live in and the desires of our flesh and sinful nature, it is impossible to avoid all contamination. There are no perfect parents on this earth. We need to be aware of this and do our best to limit the contamination as best we are able, because our kids, as much as we might love them and adore them, are not "good."

Others object to my education recommendations by saying, "Wait a minute! Don't homeschooling and Christian schools force Christianity down their throats?" Sadly, I have had people tell me from time to time that their parents harshly imposed Christianity on them, causing them to reject it. "I'm not going to force religion on my kids," they assert.

In every instance where I've talked to people who have been hurt like that, Christianity was imposed legalistically from the "top down," through pressure (and sometimes power trips) where the parent tried to make themselves the ultimate authority, rather than the Bible. When parents humbly start with the Word of God and build "from the foundation up," starting with the logical foundations of all the doctrine in Genesis, not trying to prove the Bible with science, but using the Bible to understand science, and teaching children how to defend the faith by giving them answers to skeptical questions of the age — then it makes a world of difference.

Christianity then is presented as a logical and defensible faith that makes sense of the world and is confirmed by real observational science, instead of what seems to be just a collection of opinions.

This is how we need to teach our children — from the time they are born until the time they leave home.

Parents are to train children in the truth of Scripture, giving no options. For a Christian, it is not that truth is the *best* policy (as if it were one of several acceptable alternatives). No, truth is the *only* policy. Children who are merely *taught* can hear other teaching and easily depart from the truth because of their sinful flesh and their bias against God as expressed in their fallen nature. Thus, to cause children to be influenced for good, much work must be done. We must diligently *train* them in truth, exposing and condemning error for what it is. In Paul's letter to the Ephesians, he brings up another element that reduces the risk of legalism. Consider verse 4:15:

> Rather, speaking the truth in love, we are to grow up in every way into him, who is the head, into Christ.

In 1 Corinthians 13:4–7, Paul describes this "love" in detail:

> Love is patient, love is kind . . . is not arrogant, does not act unbecomingly . . . is not provoked . . . bears all things, believes all things, hopes all things, endures all things (NASB).

I would propose to anyone who has legalistic concerns about homeschooling, that when the truth is taught in an environment of this kind of love, kids will never feel like Christianity is being forced upon them. In fact, I believe the home is the *best* environment for children to experience this kind of love from the parent, even as they learn to fulfill the greatest commandment in all of Scripture:

> You shall love the LORD your God with all your heart and
> with all your soul and with all your might (Deut. 6:5).

That love becomes the basis for the "teaching . . . talking . . . and walking" we saw earlier in this passage.

Even when homeschooling or a private Christian education seem like the best options, however, circumstances can make it impossible. Allocating the time and finances for homeschooling can be difficult for single-parent families. Many families depend on a dual income, and still don't have enough for tuition at a private Christian school. In other situations, there might be disagreement between parents when either the father or mother is not a Christian. It's also possible that a solid Christian school doesn't exist in your area, or maybe you live in a country where homeschooling resources are very, very limited (or you live in a country where homeschooling is illegal). These are all serious struggles, and reflect the fact that we certainly live in a fallen world where difficulty is a part of life.

If you are one of the people in this category, the fundamentals still apply. You may have to work harder than others and you may have to access more help, but you have the same responsibility to provide foundational scriptural instruction to your children. You have the responsibility to belong to a strong Bible-believing and teaching church, and you have the responsibility to manage the circles of influence that your children are exposed to. If you have no option but for your children to be educated in the secular system, then you must acknowledge that the responsibility of the position you hold has just been magnified, and therefore checking homework and monitoring your children's friendships will be of the utmost importance.

Always remember that it is your responsibility, within your means, to see that your child is trained and educated according to biblical principles.

God is a gracious God and forgives, but the consequences of your actions will still be part of the legacy you leave . . . and you only have one opportunity to leave it, so you better be sure you're doing it as you should. If God's people do not produce godly offspring, then the application of the truth of God's Word will be severely and negatively impacted for generations to come or to the world around. Who then will be our evangelists, pastors, missionaries, Christian teachers, and Sunday school teachers?

Remember, as said earlier, every child conceived in a mother's womb is a being who will live forever in heaven or hell! And each child is a gift from God entrusted to parents to train! As parents, we will be held accountable by our Creator God. How will each of us stand up to this accountability?

Our whole Western world is changing. But really, it's the failure of so many Christian homes and churches who have not understood the times, have not stood uncompromisingly on the authority of the Word of God, and have not trained coming generations in a Christian world-view. Yes, it only takes one generation to lose a culture. That is happening right now in America and across the Western world. In many countries it has already happened.

Who has the courage to stand up and challenge homes and churches concerning the reality of what has been happening to generations of children and now the dramatic changes in the 20s generation?

As one person in his 20s said to me, "The loss of the 20s generation is really in many ways a failure of the previous generations in our homes and churches."

I agree!

So, are you ready to return? Will you help this generation return to God? If so, let's join together and fight for their souls. Much is at stake, and the time is right now!

Afterword

Over the years, I've had many parents/grandparents approach me after I have given a presentation dealing with the issues detailed in this book. Their comments typically are as follows. "We recognize the problems and admit we didn't train our children like we should have. We tried to teach them to defend their faith but in reality allowed the public education system and their peers to train and influence them. Now what can we do?" Some of them tell me their kids no longer go to church, or the grandkids have nothing to do with church. A number of these people are quite distraught as they talk to me — some even sobbing.

So what *can* we do? Here's my counsel to those struggling with this issue:

1. We have to admit that we can't go back to redo the training of our children. And if there's been a lack of training on our part as parents, there will be consequences, not only in the children, but also in generations to come — negative consequences. So we have to be willing to acknowledge that. Scripture is clear that children are not punished nor do they bear the guilt of their parents' sins.

Moses wrote,

> Fathers shall not be put to death because of their children, nor shall children be put to death because of their fathers. Each one shall be put to death for his own sin (Deut. 24:16).

The Prophet Ezekiel records,

> Yet you say, "Why should not the son suffer for the iniquity of the father?" When the son has done what is just and right, and has been careful to observe all my statutes, he shall surely live. The soul who sins shall die. The son shall not suffer for the iniquity of the father, nor the father suffer for the iniquity of the son. The righteousness of the righteous shall be upon himself, and the wickedness of the wicked shall be upon himself.
>
> But if a wicked person turns away from all his sins that he has committed and keeps all my statutes and does what is just and right, he shall surely live; he shall not die. None of the transgressions that he has committed shall be remembered against him; for the righteousness that he has done he shall live. Have I any pleasure in the death of the wicked, declares the Lord GOD, and not rather that he should turn from his way and live? But when a righteous person turns away from his righteousness and does injustice and does the same abominations that the wicked person does, shall he live? None of the righteous deeds that he has done shall be remembered; for the treachery of which he is guilty and the sin he has committed, for them he shall die (Ezek. 18:19–24).

However, this does not mean there aren't natural and spiritual ripple effects resulting from negligent or faulty parenting. As the Lord told Israel,

> You shall not bow down to them or serve [idols], for I the LORD your God am a jealous God, visiting the iniquity of the fathers on the children to the third and the fourth generation of those who hate me, but showing steadfast love to thousands of those who love me and keep my commandments (Exod. 20:5–6).

The undeniable truth is that every child is a product of a home and the parenting practiced in that home. Each day, we as parents impact our children, for good or for bad. This is not to say that our children will automatically become godly adults, as each person must make their own spiritual choices. But it is to say that the influence a parent exerts on a child, whether good or bad, is felt for a lifetime — or *even for generations*.

2. I believe it's important to acknowledge this problem before the Lord and seek forgiveness from Him. And He is a God who forgives. However, even with forgiveness, we may still experience the hurt of seeing the negative consequences of our previous actions before our eyes. Nonetheless, we need to know God has forgiven when there is true repentance and then work to rectify the situation as best as we are able. For the believer in Jesus, failure is never final. And Scripture's heroes are living proof that it is never too late to get right before God.

3. In many instances, I believe the fathers will have to admit to their families that they did not carry out their God-commanded responsibilities to be the spiritual head of the house. The father should ask forgiveness from his family and pray that through this example of reconciliation his adult children would be pointed to Christ. After all, God honors a "broken and contrite heart."

The sacrifices of God are a broken spirit; a broken and contrite heart, O God, you will not despise (Ps. 51:17).

Depending on many circumstances, a dad could sit down with each child and explain how he now sees things and admit he should have done things very differently in regard to their upbringing. He should let them know he has confessed this to the Lord and then ask them to forgive him too (even if they don't even understand what this means right now). Sometimes the prodigal is not the son, but rather the father.

4. Determine going forward that you will be an example to them of what a good father (or mother) can be. The best way to do this is through practical illustrations of love for them in the circumstances they are in. It may be through being a great grandparent or by relating to your children as adults, being an encouragement to them in tangible ways.

5. In meekness and gentleness, begin offering apologetics resources (books, DVDs) for them and their children for birthdays, Christmas, or just for no reason at all. Sponsor a trip to the Creation Museum and Ark Encounter (and other biblically based facilities like Sight and Sound). Go with them on the zip lines at the Creation Museum. I've met many grandparents who paid to bring their grandkids (and kids) to the Creation Museum, giving them a great vacation as well as visiting other places (e.g., theme parks, zoos, aquariums, etc.). This can be a great time for bonding, and with the Creation Museum mixed in with other places, also a time for sharing the truth of God's Word without preaching to them. This is a practical way those with adult children can still "make a defense to anyone who asks you for a reason for the hope that is in you; yet do it with gentleness and respect" (1 Pet. 3:15).

6. Spend much time in prayer with your spouse for your children, grandchildren, and the generations to come. Prayer is the source of our power, and according to James is effective when offered by the one who has confessed his sins.

Therefore, confess your sins to one another and pray for one another, that you may be healed. The prayer of a righteous person has great power as it is working (James 5:16).

Appendix A

The Survey

Denomination Comparative

As part of the research America's Research Group conducted on the state of the church, those responding were asked to give what denomination they belonged to. These statistics are very revealing in a number of ways:

1. When those who indicated they were Catholic were removed, the overall results for the other denominations remained essentially the same!

2. The largest Protestant denomination in the USA is the Baptist group. The results showed that overall, the 20's group in the Baptists was not as bad as other denominations, but the same inherent problems are present nonetheless.

The following includes many of the detailed questions and responses that contain a wealth of information that would take another book to discuss. As you study this denominational comparative, no doubt it will provoke much discussion and more questions. The bottom line is that there is a problem throughout church denominations that needs to be addressed. There is no doubt many even in the most conservative churches need in-depth Bible and apologetics teaching.

An Important Note About the Data

To properly understand this set of comparative aggregates — you are looking at 6 columns of data for 20-year-olds based upon which church they currently attend.

We used question 2 to create these 6 sets of results.

When reviewing these findings, you need to examine the answers vertically.

For example: look at question #8, you will see 68.7% of Baptists consider themselves born again while only 35.8% of Catholics describe themselves that way. And on Question #26, 33% of Methodists believe other books like the Koran are inspired by God, while only 11.5% of non-denominationals feel that way.

Q1: Age?

	Baptist	Catholic	Non-denominational	Methodist	Church of Christ	Presbyt. USA
25–29	49.7	62.5	60.6	53.0	60.0	51.0
20–24	50.3	37.5	39.4	47.0	40.0	49.0

Q2: Which church denomination do you primarily attend?

	Baptist	Catholic	Non-den.	Methodist	Ch. of Christ	Presbyt. USA
Baptist Church	100.0	0.0	0.0	0.0	0.0	0.0
Catholic	0.0	100.0	0.0	0.0	0.0	0.0
Non-denominational	0.0	0.0	100.0	0.0	0.0	0.0
Methodist	0.0	0.0	0.0	100.0	0.0	0.0
Presbyterian USA	0.0	0.0	0.0	0.0	0.0	100.0
Church of Christ	0.0	0.0	0.0	0.0	100.0	0.0

Q3: How often did you attend church when you were growing up?

	Baptist	Catholic	Non-den.	Methodist	Ch. of Christ	Presbyt. USA
Most Sundays	46.9	22.5	39.4	40.0	20.0	33.3
Every week	24.6	51.7	19.2	19.0	28.6	19.6
Twice a month	11.7	10.0	14.4	19.0	31.4	17.6
Less than lx month	7.8	2.5	15.4	16.0	5.7	17.6
Never	3.9	7.5	9.6	4.0	2.9	3.9
Once a month	5.0	5.8	1.9	2.0	11.4	7.8

Q6: When you lived at home with your parents, how often did you pray together as a family?

	Baptist	Catholic	Non-den.	Methodist	Ch. of Christ	Presbyt. USA
Only at mealtime	43.6	25.0	36.5	44.0	40.0	51.0
Few times a week	16.2	30.8	15.4	20.0	8.6	25.5
Every day	17.9	31.7	16.3	9.0	25.7	7.8
Christian holidays	17.3	8.3	26.9	22.0	17.1	13.7
Once a week	5.0	4.2	4.8	5.0	8.6	2.0

Q8: Do you consider yourself born-again?

	Baptist	Catholic	Non-denom.	Methodist	Ch. of Christ	Presbyt.
Yes	68.7	35.8	69.2	47.0	48.6	37.3
No	30.2	60.0	27.9	46.0	51.4	62.7
Don't know	1.1	4.2	2.9	7.0	0.0	0.0

Q11: While living at home, to which church denomination did you belong?

	Baptist	Catholic	Non-denom.	Methodist	Church of Christ	Presbyt. USA
Baptist	85.5	0.8	12.5	0.0	17.1	7.8
Catholic	2.2	90.0	0.0	0.0	0.0	0.0
Methodist	1.7	0.0	3.8	87.0	0.0	3.9
Non-denom.	1.1	6.7	61.5	2.0	0.0	0.0
Presbyt.	0.6	0.0	1.0	0.0	0.0	76.4
Church of Christ	0.0	0.0	0.0	0.0	65.7	2.0
None	3.4	1.7	1.9	4.0	0.0	3.9
Church of God	0.6	0.0	1.0	0.0	8.6	3.9
Christian Ch.	0.0	0.0	4.8	2.0	0.0	0.0
United Church of Christ	0.6	0.8	0.0	0.0	5.7	0.0

Q12: Did you attend church regularly during your elementary and middle school years?

	Baptist	Catholic	Non-denom.	Methodist	Church of Christ	Presbyt. USA
Yes	84.4	90.0	76.6	75.0	85.7	72.5
No	15.6	10.0	24.0	25.0	14.3	27.5

Q16: Has anyone, like a friend, school teacher, or college professor, ever challenged you and your Christian faith?

	Baptist	Catholic	Non-denom.	Methodist	Church of Christ	Presbyt. USA
No	67.6	79.2	63.5	86.0	85.7	90.2
Yes	29.1	20.0	36.5	14.0	11.4	7.8
Don't know	3.4	0.8	0.0	0.0	2.9	2.0

Q17: If yes, at what time in your life were you challenged?

	Baptist	Catholic	Non-denom.	Methodist	Church of Christ	Presbyt. USA
After college	55.8	50.0	50.0	50.0	0.0	0.0
College	26.9	25.0	28.9	28.6	25.0	0.0
High school	7.7	12.5	10.5	21.4	0.0	100.0
Middle school	9.6	12.5	10.5	0.0	75.0	0.0

Q18: If yes, can you recall which specific Christian principle you were challenged on?

	Baptist	Catholic	Non-denom.	Methodist	Church of Christ	Presbyt. USA
Why bad things happen	13.5	33.3	15.8	14.3	75.0	50.0
How can believe Bible?	25.0	16.7	15.8	21.4	25.0	0.0
Age of earth	17.3	8.3	26.3	21.4	0.0	0.0
Only Christians to heaven	19.2	4.2	21.1	14.3	0.0	25.0
Can Christians be gay?	5.8	8.3	2.6	7.1	0.0	0.0
No	13.5	0.0	0.0	0.0	0.0	0.0
Creation/Garden of Eden	0.0	8.3	7.9	7.1	0.0	0.0
Why is there hell?	3.8	8.3	0.0	14.3	0.0	0.0
Virgin birth	1.9	4.2	7.9	0.0	0.0	0.0
Abortion	0.0	8.3	2.6	0.0	0.0	25.0

Q25: Do you believe all the books of the Bible are inspired by God?

	Baptist	Catholic	Non-denom.	Methodist	Church of Christ	Presbyt. USA
Yes	95.0	96.7	86.5	99.0	94.3	86.3
Don't know	3.4	1.7	8.7	0.0	0.0	7.8
No	1.7	1.7	4.8	1.0	5.7	5.9

Q26: Do you believe other holy books like the Qur'an (Koran) are inspired by God?

	Baptist	Catholic	Non-denom.	Methodist	Church of Christ	Presbyt. USA
No	72.1	68.3	82.7	51.0	71.4	62.7
Yes	16.2	26.7	11.5	33.0	28.6	11.8
Don't know	11.7	5.0	5.8	16.0	0.0	25.5

Q27: Have you ever read the Bible from cover to cover?

	Baptist	Catholic	Non-denom.	Methodist	Church of Christ	Presbyt. USA
No	78.8	74.2	76.9	80.0	82.9	84.3
Yes	20.7	23.3	23.1	19.0	17.1	15.7

Q28: If not, have you read much of the Old Testament?

	Baptist	Catholic	Non-denom.	Methodist	Church of Christ	Presbyt. USA
No	65.2	71.9	77.5	76.3	79.3	67.4
Yes	34.8	28.1	22.5	23.8	20.7	32.6

Q29: If not, have you read much of the New Testament?

	Baptist	Catholic	Non-denom.	Methodist	Church of Christ	Presbyt. USA
Yes	60.3	52.8	60.0	43.8	62.1	53.5
No	39.7	47.2	40.0	56.3	37.9	46.5

Q30: Do you believe more in creation as stated in the Bible or more in evolution?

	Baptist	Catholic	Non-denom.	Methodist	Church of Christ	Presbyt. USA
Biblical creation	88.3	91.7	76.9	71.0	82.9	58.8
Evolution	11.7	8.3	23.1	29.0	17.1	41.2

Q31: Do you feel the church is relevant today to your needs?

	Baptist	Catholic	Non-denom.	Methodist	Church of Christ	Presbyt. USA
Yes	75.4	80.8	86.5	72.0	77.1	72.5
No	20.7	13.3	12.5	25.0	20.0	25.5
Don't know	3.9	5.8	1.0	3.0	2.9	2.0

Q32: If no, in what way do you feel the church is not fulfilling your needs?

	Baptist	Catholic	Non-denom.	Methodist	Church of Christ	Presbyt. USA
Not feel closer to God	78.4	6.3	30.8	88.0	57.1	84.6
Not learn about God	2.7	62.5	23.1	0.0	14.3	7.7
Not meet emotion	0.0	31.3	15.4	4.0	0.0	7.7
Bible not practical	2.7	0.0	7.7	8.0	28.6	0.0
Don't know	16.2	0.0	0.0	0.0	0.0	0.0
Music is poor	0.0	0.0	23.1	0.0	0.0	0.0

Q33: Do you believe the bible is true and historically accurate?

	Baptist	Catholic	Non-denom.	Methodist	Church of Christ	Presbyt. USA
Yes	76.5	82.5	68.3	69.0	82.9	56.9
No	13.4	11.7	15.4	20.0	17.1	41.2
Don't know	10.1	5.8	16.3	11.0	0.0	2.0

Q34: If no, what is it that made you begin to doubt the Bible?

	Baptist	Catholic	Non-denom.	Methodist	Church of Christ	Presbyt. USA
Written by men	41.7	14.3	62.5	5.0	16.7	47.6
Science shows earth is old	16.7	21.4	18.8	10.0	16.7	19.0
Not translated correctly	12.5	7.1	0.0	45.0	0.0	9.5
Bible contradicts	25.0	14.3	12.5	10.0	0.0	4.8
Bible has errors	0.0	35.7	0.0	5.0	66.7	9.5
Evolution	0.0	0.0	6.3	20.0	0.0	0.0
Christians don't live by it	4.2	0.0	0.0	5.0	0.0	9.5
Suffering and death	0.0	7.1	0.0	0.0	0.0	0.0

Q35: If no, when did you first have doubts?

	Baptist	Catholic	Non-denom.	Methodist	Church of Christ	Presbyt. USA
Middle school	58.3	28.6	6.3	70.0	83.3	81.0
High school	29.2	35.7	50.0	10.0	0.0	9.5
Elementary school	4.2	7.1	37.5	10.0	0.0	0.0
College	4.2	28.6	6.3	5.0	16.7	4.8
Don't know	4.2	0.0	0.0	0.0	0.0	4.8
Misc	0.0	0.0	0.0	5.0	0.0	0.0

Q36: Do you believe Adam and Eve were real people in the Garden of Eden or were they fictional characters?

	Baptist	Catholic	Non-denom.	Methodist	Church of Christ	Presbyt. USA
Real	86.6	96.7	84.6	70.0	77.1	72.5
Fictional	12.8	3.3	14.4	19.0	14.3	27.5
Don't know	0.6	0.0	1.0	11.0	8.6	0.0

Q37: Do you believe Adam and Eve sinned and were expelled from the Garden?

	Baptist	Catholic	Non-denom.	Methodist	Church of Christ	Presbyt. USA
Yes	87.2	96.7	84.6	74.0	80.0	72.5
No	12.8	3.3	9.6	19.0	17.1	27.5
Don't know	0.0	0.0	5.8	7.0	2.9	0.0

Q38: Do you believe in the account of Sodom and Gomorrah and that Lot's wife was turned to salt when she looked back at the city?

	Baptist	Catholic	Non-denom.	Methodist	Church of Christ	Presbyt. USA
Yes	79.3	70.8	75.0	68.0	74.3	56.9
No	11.7	5.8	12.5	23.0	20.0	33.3
Don't know	8.9	23.3	12.5	9.0	5.7	9.8

Q39: Do you believe in Noah's ark and the global Flood?

	Baptist	Catholic	Non-denom.	Methodist	Church of Christ	Presbyt. USA
Yes	88.3	97.5	81.7	89.0	91.4	86.3
No	10.6	1.7	18.3	9.0	5.7	11.8

Q40: Do you believe in the birth of Isaac when Abraham was about 100 years old?

	Baptist	Catholic	Non-denom.	Methodist	Church of Christ	Presbyt. USA
Yes	79.3	71.7	76.9	86.0	77.1	66.7
Don't know	14.0	23.3	7.7	3.0	2.9	21.6
No	6.7	5.0	15.4	11.0	20.0	11.8

Q41: Some biblical scholars estimate the earth to be 6,000 years old, and other biblical scholars estimate the earth to be 10,000 years old. Which one do you believe?

	Baptist	Catholic	Non-denom.	Methodist	Church of Christ	Presbyt. USA
Neither	38.0	50.0	56.7	59.0	42.9	56.9
IOK years old	43.0	36.7	30.8	35.0	57.1	29.4
6K years old	19.0	13.3	12.5	6.0	0.0	13.7

Q42: Do you believe God created universe, the heavens, and earth in 24-hour days or do you believe those days were much longer than 24 hours?

	Baptist	Catholic	Non-denom.	Methodist	Church of Christ	Presbyt. USA
Actual 24 hours	71.5	66.7	53.8	59.0	80.0	58.8
Longer than 24 hours	27.9	33.3	45.2	41.0	20.0	41.2

Q43: Do you believe God is truly almighty, holy, and full of love?

	Baptist	Catholic	Non-denom.	Methodist	Church of Christ	Presbyt. USA
Yes	99.4	100.0	99.0	99.0	100.0	100.0

Q44: Do you believe God truly inspired each of the authors of the various books of the Bible?

	Baptist	Catholic	Non-denom.	Methodist	Church of Christ	Presbyt. USA
Yes	91.1	96.7	81.7	89.0	91.4	92.2
No	3.9	3.3	18.3	10.0	5.7	5.9
Don't know	5.0	0.0	0.0	1.0	2.9	2.0

Q45: Do you believe that dinosaurs died out before people were on the planet?

	Baptist	Catholic	Non-denom.	Methodist	Church of Christ	Presbyt. USA
Yes	53.1	47.5	55.8	47.0	68.6	60.8
Don't know	29.6	24.2	25.0	23.0	14.3	17.6
No	17.3	28.3	19.2	30.0	17.1	21.6

Q46: Which do you believe — secular science which has dated the earth at billions of years old, or the Bible which teaches the world was created in six 24-hour days?

	Baptist	Catholic	Non-denom.	Methodist	Church of Christ	Presbyt. USA
Six 24-hr days	75.4	69.2	60.6	62.0	77.1	47.1
Billions of years	24.6	30.8	39.4	38.0	22.9	52.9

Q47: Do you believe that God used evolution to change one kind of animal into another kind (e.g., the evolutionary belief that dinosaurs evolved into birds)?

	Baptist	Catholic	Non-denom.	Methodist	Church of Christ	Presbyt. USA
No	76.0	80.8	63.5	60.0	68.6	45.1
Yes	16.8	15.8	32.7	33.0	17.1	43.l
Don't know	7.3	3.3	3.8	7.0	14.3	11.8

Q48: Do you believe that humans evolved from ape- like ancestors?

	Baptist	Catholic	Non-denom.	Methodist	Church of Christ	Presbyt. USA
No	78.8	83.3	76.0	68.0	71.4	54.9
Yes	14.5	10.0	22.1	24.0	22.9	27.5
Don't know	6.7	6.7	1.9	8.0	5.7	17.6

Q49: When you were younger, did your pastor ever preach on Darwinism and why it is not true and should not be believed?

	Baptist	Catholic	Non-denom.	Methodist	Church of Christ	Presbyt. USA
No	61.5	74.2	65.4	64.0	68.6	56.9
Yes	29.1	17.5	11.5	21.0	22.9	27.5
Don't know	9.5	8.3	23.1	15.0	8.6	15.7

Q50: When you were younger and listening to your minister's sermon, do you recall him preaching about Adam and Eve, evolution, or the number of days in which God created the heaven and earth?

	Baptist	Catholic	Non-denom.	Methodist	Church of Christ	Presbyt. USA
Yes	77.7	88.3	71.2	78.0	77.1	70.6
No	15.1	8.3	25.0	21.0	17.1	17.6
Don't know	7.3	3.3	3.8	1.0	5.7	11.8

Q51: Have you ever had anyone, your minister, your Sunday school teacher, your youth pastor, or your youth leader teach you how to defend your Christian faith if ever challenged in the future?

	Baptist	Catholic	Non-denom.	Methodist	Church of Christ	Presbyt. USA
Yes	49.2	70.0	44.2	44.0	42.9	27.5
No	47.5	25.0	53.8	50.0	54.3	72.5
Don't know	3.4	5.0	1.9	6.0	2.9	0.0

Q53: Did your pastor ever teach that Christians could believe in an earth that is millions or billions of years old?

	Baptist	Catholic	Non-denom.	Methodist	Church of Christ	Presbyt. USA
No	69.8	65.0	56.7	71.0	54.3	47.1
Yes	14.0	20.0	31.7	20.0	20.0	33.3
Don't know	16.2	15.0	11.5	9.0	25.7	19.6

Q54: Did your pastor teach that God created the earth in six days, each 24 hours in length?

	Baptist	Catholic	Non-denom.	Methodist	Church of Christ	Presbyt. USA
Yes	76.5	82.5	71.2	73.0	80.0	70.6
No	13.4	16.7	24.0	14.0	14.3	7.8
Don't know	10.1	0.8	4.8	13.0	5.7	21.6

Q55: Did your pastor ever say anything to make you believe the Book of Genesis contained many myths and legends that we now know are untrue?

	Baptist	Catholic	Non-denom.	Methodist	Church of Christ	Presbyt. USA
No	82.7	89.2	86.5	76.0	88.6	56.9
Yes	11.2	9.2	12.5	23.0	5.7	39.2
Don't know	6.1	1.7	1.0	1.0	5.7	3.9

Q56: Do you believe in Joseph being sold into slavery and later becoming the pharaoh's closest advisor and eventually seeing his brothers?

	Baptist	Catholic	Non-denom.	Methodist	Church of Christ	Presbyt. USA.
Yes	76.5	76.7	76.0	76.0	65.7	68.6
Don't know	21.2	17.5	16.3	22.0	31.4	29.4
No	2.2	5.8	7.7	2.0	2.9	2.0

Q60: Do you have children or plan to have children in the future?

	Baptist	Catholic	Non-denom.	Methodist	Church of Christ	Presbyt. USA
Have	60.9	46.7	50.0	42.0	60.0	25.5
Plan to	25.1	42.5	25.0	48.0	34.3	56.9
No	11.7	7.5	22.1	6.0	2.9	15.7
Don't know	2.2	3.3	2.9	4.0	2.9	2.0

Q61: If you have children, are you taking them or encouraging them to go to church?

	Baptist	Catholic	Non-denom.	Methodist	Church of Christ	Presbyt. USA
Yes	88.1	98.2	96.2	88.1	100.0	92.3
No	10.1	0.0	3.8	9.5	0.0	7.7

Q62: If you plan to have children, do you plan to take them to church?

	Baptist	Catholic	Non-denom.	Methodist	Church of Christ	Presbyt. USA
Yes	68.9	74.5	96.2	68.8	50.0	79.3
Don't know	31.1	25.5	3.8	31.3	16.7	20.7
No	0.0	0.0	0.0	0.0	33.3	0.0

Q63: If you have children or plan to, how important is it to you to attend church regularly as a family?

	Baptist	Catholic	Non-denom.	Methodist	Church of Christ	Presbyt. USA
Very important	28.6	40.2	33.3	34.4	27.3	21.4
Important	20.8	37.4	41.0	32.2	21.2	19.0
Extremely important	36.4	20.6	21.8	12.2	33.3	38.I
Somewhat important	12.3	1.9	3.8	14.4	6.1	21.4
Little/no importance	1.9	0.0	0.0	6.7	12.1	0.0

Q64: Do you attend any church services at Easter or Christmas?

	Baptist	Catholic	Non-denom.	Methodist	Church of Christ	Presbyt. USA
Both	65.4	65.0	75.0	56.0	62.9	72.5
Christmas	16.2	15.0	12.5	24.0	8.6	7.8
No	12.8	14.2	4.8	17.0	20.0	17.6
Easter	5.6	5.8	7.7	3.0	8.6	2.0

Q65: In elementary school, did you primarily attend public school, Christian school, charter school, home school, or Catholic/parochial school?

	Baptist	Catholic	Non-denom.	Methodist	Church of Christ	Presbyt. USA
Public school	86.6	60.0	89.4	97.0	100.0	94.1
Christian school	10.1	7.5	6.7	3.0	0.0	3.9
Catholic-parochial	0.0	31.7	0.0	0.0	0.0	0.0
Charter school	0.6	0.0	3.8	0.0	0.0	0.0

Q66: In high school, did you primarily attend public school, Christian school, charter school, home school, or Catholic/parochial school?

	Baptist	Catholic	Non-denom.	Methodist	Church of Christ	Presbyt. USA
Public school	87.7	78.3	90.4	97.0	100.0	94.1
Christian school	9.5	5.8	4.8	3.0	0.0	3.9
Catholic-parochial	0.0	15.8	0.0	0.0	0.0	0.0
Charter school	0.6	0.0	4.8	0.0	0.0	0.0

Q67: Did your science teachers teach you the earth was millions or billions of years old?

	Baptist	Catholic	Non-denom.	Methodist	Church of Christ	Presbyt. USA
Yes	85.5	83.3	86.5	88.0	91.4	74.5
No	11.2	14.2	12.5	10.0	5.7	23.5
Don't know	3.4	2.5	1.0	2.0	2.9	2.0

Q68: Did any of your schoolteachers teach you that humans definitely evolved from lower forms of life to become what they are today?

	Baptist	Catholic	Non-denom.	Methodist	Church of Christ	Presbyt. USA
Yes	73.2	55.0	71.2	65.0	62.9	62.7
No	24.6	40.0	25.0	32.0	17.1	37.3
Don't know	2.2	5.0	3.8	3.0	20.0	0.0

Q69: By the time you graduated from high school, did you believe that the Bible was less true?

	Baptist	Catholic	Non-denom.	Methodist	Church of Christ	Presbyt. USA
No	76.0	87.5	80.8	67.0	71.4	66.7
Yes	18.4	10.8	14.4	29.0	25.7	27.5
Don't know	5.6	1.7	4.8	4.0	2.9	5.9

Q70: If yes, which person or persons convinced you the most that the Bible was less true?

	Baptist	Catholic	Non-denom.	Methodist	Church of Christ	Presbyt. USA
Hgh school teacher	57.6	69.2	73.3	24.1	33.3	92.9
Teenage friends	30.3	23.1	13.3	48.3	66.7	7.1
Adult friends	12.1	7.7	13.3	27.6	0.0	0.0

Q71: Does the Bible contain errors?

	Baptist	Catholic	Non-denom.	Methodist	Church of Christ	Presbyt. USA
No	73.2	82.5	45.2	62.0	65.7	33.3
Yes	14.0	12.5	30.8	32.0	17.1	56.9
Don't know	12.8	5.0	24.0	6.0	17.1	9.8

Q72: If yes, can you identify one of those errors for me?

	Baptist	Catholic	Non-denom.	Methodist	Church of Christ	Presbyt. USA
Wrong about age	52.0	20.0	43.8	46.9	33.3	27.6
Writers made mistakes	40.0	26.7	21.9	37.5	66.7	55.2
Alleged contradiction	0.0	26.7	25.0	3.1	0.0	0.0
Genesis disproved	4.0	6.7	6.3	3.1	0.0	13.8
No flood in Noah's tme	4.0	6.7	3.1	6.3	0.0	0.0
Unsaved go to hell	0.0	13.3	0.0	0.0	0.0	0.0
Miracles didn't occur	0.0	0.0	0.0	3.1	0.0	0.0
No	0.0	0.0	0.0	0.0	0.0	3.4

Q77: Do you feel good people don't need to go to church?

	Baptist	Catholic	Non-denom.	Methodist	Church of Christ	Presbyt. USA
No	69.8	60.8	81.7	58.0	71.4	60.8
Yes	26.8	35.8	11.5	34.0	25.7	35.3
Don't know	3.4	3.3	6.7	8.0	2.9	3.9

Q78: Do you feel people with a college education are less likely to attend church because they have been greatly influenced by professors who taught them the Bible was not reliable and was not the Word of God?

	Baptist	Catholic	Non-denom.	Methodist	Church of Christ	Presbyt. USA
No	45.8	71.7	42.3	52.0	65.7	58.8
Yes	38.0	15.0	29.8	28.0	28.6	27.5
Don't know	16.2	13.3	27.9	20.0	5.7	13.7

Q79: Do you believe if you are a good person you will go to heaven upon your death?

	Baptist	Catholic	Non-denom.	Methodist	Church of Christ	Presbyt. USA
Yes	49.2	70.8	64.4	63.0	65.7	76.5
No	48.0	20.0	34.6	32.0	28.6	21.6
Don't know	2.8	9.2	1.0	5.0	5.7	2.0

Q81: Do you believe only those who have received Christ as their Lord and Savior will go to heaven?

	Baptist	Catholic	Non-denom.	Methodist	Church of Christ	Presbyt. USA
Yes	71.5	53.3	52.9	49.0	51.4	47.1
No	25.7	44.2	23.1	28.0	25.7	31.4
Don't know	2.8	2.5	24.0	23.0	22.9	21.6

Q82: Do you believe you have become anti-church through the years?

	Baptist	Catholic	Non-denom.	Methodist	Church of Christ	Presbyt. USA
No	81.6	80.0	85.6	77.0	74.3	96.1
Yes	15.6	17.5	12.5	11.0	25.7	2.0
Don't know	2.8	2.5	1.9	12.0	0.0	2.0

Q83: Of these choices, which one makes you question the Bible the most?

	Baptist	Catholic	Non-denom.	Methodist	Church of Christ	Presbyt. USA
None	63.1	60.0	42.3	47.0	48.6	31.4
Age of earth can't be less than 10K	12.8	19.2	26.9	26.0	8.6	43.1
Too many rules	8.9	5.0	9.6	10.0	22.9	5.9
No sense in suffering/death	6.1	5.0	11.5	10.0	14.3	2.0
Creation account	6.1	5.0	2.9	4.0	5.7	17.6
Worldwide flood	1.1	4.2	3.8	2.0	0.0	0.0

Q84: Which of these best describes your belief — the Bible is the Word of God written down by men who God inspired, or the Bible is a book that many men wrote years ago and it is simply a collection of writings by wise men?

	Baptist	Catholic	Non-denom.	Methodist	Church of Christ	Presbyt. USA
Bible is the Word of God	78.8	91.7	77.9	69.0	74.3	64.7
Bible is a collection of writings	21.2	7.5	22.1	31.0	25.7	35.3

Q85: Should gay couples be allowed to marry and have all the legal rights of heterosexual couples?

	Baptist	Catholic	Non-denom.	Methodist	Church of Christ	Presbyt. USA
No	64.8	42.5	44.2	30.0	40.0	33.3
Yes	23.5	48.3	51.0	58.0	31.4	47.1
Don't know	11.7	9.2	4.8	11.0	28.6	19.6

Q86: Is homosexual behavior a sin?

	Baptist	Catholic	Non-denom.	Methodist	Church of Christ	Presbyt. USA
Yes	67.6	60.0	53.8	39.0	74.3	35.3
No	21.2	25.0	31.7	44.0	14.3	41.2
Don't know	11.2	15.0	14.4	16.0	11.4	23.5

Q87: Should abortions continue to be legal in most instances?

	Baptist	Catholic	Non-denom.	Methodist	Church of Christ	Presbyt. USA.
No	60.9	45.8	44.2	38.0	62.9	39.2
Yes	27.4	29.2	46.2	47.0	28.6	23.5
Don't know	11.7	25.0	9.6	14.0	8.6	37.3

Q88: Should marijuana be allowed for persons with certain medical conditions?

	Baptist	Catholic	Non-denom.	Methodist	Church of Christ	Presbyt. USA
Yes	64.2	72.5	72.1	77.0	77.1	68.6
No	22.3	18.3	12.5	16.0	11.4	5.9
Don't know	13.4	9.2	15.4	7.0	11.4	25.5

Q89: Should marijuana be made legal all across America?

	Baptist	Catholic	Non-denom.	Methodist	Church of Christ	Presbyt. USA
No	68.2	51.7	52.9	40.0	48.6	60.8
Yes	27.9	45.0	43.3	51.0	45.7	25.5
Don't know	3.9	3.3	3.8	9.0	5.7	13.7

Q90: Should science instructors be allowed to teach the problems with evolution or strictly teach about evolution?

	Baptist	Catholic	Non-denom.	Methodist	Church of Christ	Presbyt. USA
Allow to teach problems	92.7	88.3	80.8	90.0	97.1	92.2
Strictly teach	7.3	9.2	19.2	10.0	2.9	7.8

Q91: Should prayer be allowed in public schools?

	Baptist	Catholic	Non-denom.	Methodist	Church of Christ	Presbyt. USA
Yes	91.1	77.5	82.7	88.0	91.4	88.2
No	7.3	8.3	13.5	9.0	5.7	5.9
Don't know	1.7	14.2	3.8	3.0	2.9	5.9

Q92: Do you believe many of the problems facing public schools are a result of taking God out of the classroom and out of the school?

	Baptist	Catholic	Non-denom.	Methodist	Church of Christ	Presbyt. USA
Yes	72.6	60.0	67.3	48.0	71.4	54.9
No	23.5	37.5	24.0	31.0	25.7	31.4
Don't know	3.9	2.5	8.7	21.0	2.9	13.7

Q93: Is premarital sex okay?

	Baptist	Catholic	Non-denom.	Methodist	Church of Christ	Presbyt. USA
No	62.0	60.0	43.3	33.0	60.0	35.3
Yes	33.5	25.0	55.8	52.0	31.4	47.1
Don't know	4.5	15.0	1.0	14.0	8.6	17.6

Q94: Should smoking marijuana be made legal?

	Baptist	Catholic	Non-denom.	Methodist	Church of Christ	Presbyt. USA
No	68.2	50.8	53.8	34.0	40.0	43.1
Yes	27.9	35.0	44.2	53.0	48.6	27.5
Don't know	3.9	14.2	1.9	13.0	11.4	29.4

Q95: Do you believe the Church is too judgmental and discriminates against those who don't attend?

	Baptist	Catholic	Non-denom.	Methodist	Church of Christ	Presbyt. USA
No	54.7	51.7	50.0	42.0	42.9	31.4
Yes	29.1	41.7	33.7	39.0	25.7	39.2
Don't know	16.2	6.7	16.3	19.0	31.4	29.4

Q96: Who smashed the tablets on which God had written the 10 Commandments?

	Baptist	Catholic	Non-denom.	Methodist	Church of Christ	Presbyt. USA
Moses	74.9	74.2	61.5	70.0	57.1	62.7
Don't know	21. 2	23.3	31.7	20.0	28.6	35.3
David	2.8	0.0	4.8	6.0	14.3	0.0

Q97: What is the first book in the New Testament?

	Baptist	Catholic	Non-denom.	Methodist	Church of Christ	Presbyt. USA
Matthew	71.5	83.3	69.2	66.0	62.9	66.7
Don't know	24.6	10.0	27.9	29.0	34.3	33.3
Genesis	3.9	3.3	2.9	5.0	2.9	0.0

Q98: Who baptized Jesus?

	Baptist	Catholic	Non-denom.	Methodist	Church of Christ	Presbyt. USA
John the Baptist	82.1	76.7	75.0	71.0	68.6	70.6
Don't know	15.1	19.2	14.4	28. 0	31.4	27.5
John	1.1	2.5	4.8	1.0	0.0	2.0
Moses	0.6	0.0	5.8	0.0	0.0	0.0

Q99: Who built the ship known as the ark?

	Baptist	Catholic	Non-denom.	Methodist	Church of Christ	Presbyt. USA
Noah	91.6	88.3	90.4	94.0	85.7	94.1
Don't know	7.8	9.2	8.7	6.0	5.7	3.9
Moses	0.6	2.5	1.0	0.0	5.7	2.0

Q100: What king wrote most of the Psalms?

	Baptist	Catholic	Non-denom.	Methodist	Church of Christ	Presbyt. USA.
Don't know	43.0	35.8	52.9	57.0	57.1	49.0
David	49.2	52.5	32.7	35.0	31.4	37.3
Solomon	2.8	5.8	3.8	4.0	2.9	2.0
Luke	2.8	2.5	1.0	1.0	5.7	7.8
Jacob	0.0	0.8	8.7	0.0	2.9	0.0
John	0.0	0.0	0.0	3.0	0.0	3.9

Q101: In what town was Jesus born?

	Baptist	Catholic	Non-denom.	Methodist	Church of Christ	Presbyt. USA
Bethlehem	94.4	97.5	81.7	95.0	88.6	98.0
Jerusalem	2.2	1.7	8.7	3.0	8.6	0.0
Don't know	2.8	0.8	6.7	2.0	2.9	2.0

Q102: Did you ever memorize the names of the books of Bible in order?

	Baptist	Catholic	Non-denom.	Methodist	Church of Christ	Presbyt. USA
No	52.0	75.0	63.5	61.0	54.3	76.5
Yes	47.5	24.2	36.5	39.0	45.7	23.5

Q103: Did you memorize many verses of the Bible?

	Baptist	Catholic	Non-denom.	Methodist	Church of Christ	Presbyt. USA
Yes	68.7	52.5	70.2	63.0	65.7	68.6
No	30.2	45.8	29.8	36.0	34.3	31.4

Q104: What is your family status?

	Baptist	Catholic	Non-denom.	Methodist	Church of Christ	Presbyt. USA
Married/children	48.0	45.0	38.5	38.0	51.4	21.6
Single	27.4	28.3	35.6	35.0	31.4	35.3
Married	16.2	22.5	16.3	23.0	8.6	35.3
Single/children	6.7	1.7	7.7	3.0	8.6	3.9
Married/children away	1.7	2.5	1.9	1.0	0.0	3.9

Q106: What is the last grade of school you have completed?

	Baptist	Catholic	Non-denom.	Methodist	Church of Christ	Presbyt. USA
Some college	45.8	29.2	31.7	43.0	31.4	43.1
HS graduate	33.0	38.3	35.6	27.0	37.1	15.7
College graduate	19.0	32.5	26.9	23.0	31.4	35.3
Graduate school	1.1	0.0	4.8	7.0	0.0	5.9

Q109: Your sex?

	Baptist	Catholic	Non-denom.	Methodist	Church of Christ	Presbyt. USA
Female	74.9	65.0	65.4	76.0	68.6	60.8
Male	25.1	35.0	34.6	24.0	31.4	39.2

Gay Marriage and the 21st Century

A Fundamental Change in the Western World

Most people have heard of the story of Pandora's box. (Apparently the original myth was about Pandora's jar, but it's commonly known as Pandora's box.) Just as there are Flood legends around the world, there are also other legends with elements similar to Genesis. One of those is the legend of Pandora's box. The story claims the pagan god Zeus gave man the first woman along with a box that had a warning not to open it. But Pandora chose to open it, and by doing so unleashed all the evils known to man. Sounds like a spinoff account of the Fall as recorded in Genesis 3.

I believe the recent decision of the Supreme Court of the United States (SCOTUS) to legalize gay "marriage" has, in a sense, opened Pandora's box. Consider just a few of the headlines that appeared shortly after their decision to give you an idea what has now been unleashed on our culture:

- Polygamy Attorney On Gay Marriage Decision: SCOTUS Opinion "Resonates With Our Arguments"[1]

- Next frontier for gays is employment and housing discrimination[2]

- How Will the U.S. Supreme Court's Same-Sex-Marriage Decision Affect Religious Liberty?[3]

- Now's the Time to End Tax Exemptions for Religious Institutions[4]

- It's Time to Legalize Polygamy[5]

Pandora's Box indeed. Of course, it remains to be seen how and to what degree these agendas will be pursued. And though no gay "marriage" has the ability to naturally procreate, the above examples prove it has already birthed an odious offspring.

Mike Johnson is chief counsel of Freedom Guard, a nonprofit, constitutional law organization that has assisted Answers in Genesis with its Ark Encounter project. He says of the SCOTUS decision:

> Millions of Americans are also rightly concerned about what might happen if these critical boundaries on marriage are erased. The federal district court judge in our successful case last year asked some important questions of our opposing counsel that they could not answer. He asked the plaintiffs' attorneys: if they are correct — that the State has no authority to regulate marriage — then where could we then draw the line? Would first cousins have the right to marry? A father and his daughter? An uncle and his nephew? A 20-year-old man and a

1. http://dailycaller.com/2015/06/26/polygamy-attorney-on-gay-marriage-decision-scotus-opinion-resonates-with-our-arguments/

2. http://www.latimes.com/nation/la-na-gays-employment-20150626-story.html#page=1

3. http://www.theatlantic.com/politics/archive/2015/06/how-will-the-us-supreme-courts-same-sex-marriage-decision-affect-religious-liberty/396986/

4. http://time.com/3939143/nows-the-time-to-end-tax-exemptions-for-religious-institutions/

5. http://www.politico.com/magazine/story/2015/06/gay-marriage-decision-polygamy-119469.html?ml=po#.VbIq6HjbDRo

13-year-old girl? If the "right to marry" is determined to have no rational boundary, chaos is certain to follow. And all of those other "interest groups" will present equally fervent arguments as to why THEIR particular preferences and behaviors should be honored with equal protection under the law.[6]

This is certainly true. If marriage can be redefined on the basis of "love has no boundaries," as many people say to argue for same-sex "marriage," then where do we stop redefining marriage? Why not two men and three women? Why not a man and an animal? Where do you stop redefining marriage? It is only in God's Word that we get a standard for marriage given to us by the Creator. Marriage is for one man and one woman because God created it that way (Gen. 1:27, 2:24; Matt. 19:4-5). Since God created marriage, God — and only God — has the right to define what marriage is and is not.

As I've said many times over the years, once a worldview is built on man's opinions (man's word) and not God's Word, then, ultimately, anything goes! The best way to sum it up is from this verse of Scripture:

> In those days there was no king in Israel. Everyone did what was right in his own eyes (Judg. 21:25).

That verse is the "Pandora's box" that SCOTUS opened. In reality, this box was gradually being pried open over the years — but this latest declaration on gay "marriage" opened it widely. In an article titled, "Ending Tax Exemption means Ending Churches," one writer stated,

> Legal gay marriage is not the endgame for the gay-rights movement. It never was. Moral approval is the endgame. The agenda is not tolerance for different beliefs and lifestyles. The agenda is a demand that everyone get on board with the moral revolution or be punished. That means if you or your church won't get with the program, then the revolutionaries will endeavor to close you down.[7]

I totally agree. This is what their agenda is all about.

---

6. https://answersingenesis.org/family/marriage/supreme-court-affirms-gay-marriage/

7. http://thefederalist.com/2015/06/29/ending-tax-exemptions-means-ending-churches/.

Typically in Greek mythology, after the bad things come out, then something good also comes out. In the Bible, after the account of the Fall of man, God provides a solution in Jesus. And I'm confident God will use this SCOTUS ruling for good. Historically, persecution has been known to awaken God's people to increased fervor to serve Him and spread the gospel.

Even so, the Supreme Court ruling in favor of gay "marriage" will fundamentally change the culture in America and, apart from a miracle of God, it will prove to be an irreversible situation. To understand what is happening to America now, simply read Romans 1. Though profoundly true for Paul's day, it has proved to be prophetic for ours. I believe we're going to see increased persecution against Christians and increased antagonism specifically toward Christianity. We're going to see the restriction of the free exercise of religion, freedom of religion, and free speech in this nation, particularly with regard to our faith. Don't be surprised when you see the government move against Christian churches, colleges, institutions, and organizations that take a stand on biblical marriage as God commands in the Bible, going all the way back to the Book of Genesis.

As Jesus stated in Matthew,

> Have you not read that He who made them at the beginning "made them male and female," and said, "For this reason a man shall leave his father and mother and be joined to his wife, and the two shall become one flesh"? So then, they are no longer two but one flesh. Therefore what God has joined together, let not man separate (Matt. 19:4–6; NKJV).

Misinformation and Confusion

I must admit I have been amazed (and saddened) by the number of Christians who either completely ignore these words from Jesus or who twist and reinterpret them to fit their preferences. They also claim that because we call gay "marriage" a sin, we are being judgmental, because the Bible "tells us not to judge." Of course, many non-Christians also inconsistently quote the Bible in an attempt to prove that Christians shouldn't judge those who believe in gay "marriage."

Ironically, many of these people become judgmental themselves by making this (false) accusation. But it's not just gay "marriage" we call sin, but rather *all* sexual immorality (like adultery and fornication), along with lying, murder, and thieving, among other sins. And how dare we judge these actions as being "sin"? Because we have an absolute authority by which *all* our actions must be judged — the authority of the Word of God. God obviously is the ultimate Judge, but He has given us His Word with which to understand, discern, and judge actions. Without Scripture, we are literally left to the moral whims of the individual or the collective beliefs of a fallen society.

People regularly take Matthew 7:1 ("Judge not, that you be not judged") out of context, claiming we are not to judge. And yet that very statement becomes a judgment against those who use Scripture as a standard for morality and behavior. This is part of the inconsistent logic of unbelievers. However, when you read the whole passage carefully and in its context, Christ is actually warning believers against making judgments in a hypocritical or condemning manner. Jesus also stated in John 7:24, "Do not judge by appearances, but judge with right judgment." Notice the Lord's *command* to judge, but when doing so, we must make sure we are judging righteously from God's Word and not relying on our own human prejudice or personal opinion.

I've observed a pattern with those who disagree with the biblical stand against gay "marriage." They claim the gay "marriage" issue is all about "love" — and yet the irony escapes those who post very hateful comments against Christians and those who simply disagree with them. It appears that many who accept gay "marriage" interpret our scriptural view of not accepting their behavior as unloving and hateful. But their real goal is for everyone to accept their sinful position! However, Christians can, and do, love people with whom we disagree. And not agreeing with them and judging their position as sin based on Scripture is not being hateful or unloving! On the contrary, it's the most loving thing we can possibly do, as it helps them realize their genuine need for salvation and a Savior!

Of course, another great concern right now is that those in authority are beginning to claim that speaking against homosexual behavior or gay "marriage" is "hate speech." The president has already claimed it's a civil rights issue, even though it's clearly not. While we cannot change the shape of a person's eyes or skin shade (which are genetically determined), people can change their moral behavior. Homosexual behavior and gay "marriage" are moral issues, not genetic or civil rights issues. Still, Pandora's Box has been opened, with secularists now claiming the Bible itself is full of hate speech. How long before we are told we can't use certain passages in the Bible or we will be judged, fined, or even imprisoned for using "hate speech?" How long will we be able to have the free exercise of Christianity in this nation, as guaranteed by the U.S. Constitution?

For further information on this topic, I encourage you to read a short article I coauthored on our website titled "Does the Bible Tell Christians to Judge Not?"[8]

The Reality Behind the Reality

If you think all this sounds like war, you're right. We are currently in a battle of good versus evil, a conflict between righteousness and ungodliness — and its roots are found in the spiritual realm. Paul wrote to the Ephesians,

> For we do not wrestle against flesh and blood, but against the rulers, against the authorities, against the cosmic powers over this present darkness, against the spiritual forces of evil in the heavenly places (Eph. 6:12).

That being reality, we must primarily do battle with *spiritual* weapons. That same Apostle wisely wrote,

> For the weapons of our warfare are not of the flesh but have divine power to destroy strongholds. We destroy arguments and every lofty opinion raised against the knowledge of God, and take every thought captive to obey Christ (2 Cor. 10:4–5).

We're not fighting surface issues or physical enemies, but rather the spiritual forces behind them. Unless we keep this perspective, we can easily slip into hatred and animosity for the very people for whom Christ

---

8. https://answersingenesis.org/bible-questions/does-the-bible-tell-christians-to-judge-not/.

died. Moral and biblical conviction must always partner with compassion and the free offer of salvation to anyone who desires to call on the name of the Lord.

Gay "Marriage" Doesn't Work

Many gay "marriage" activists argue that "married" gay couples are just as suitable parents as married heterosexual couples, that there is no difference between the two. However, the president of the American College of Pediatricians, "a nonprofit organization of pediatricians and health care professionals dedicated to the health and well-being of children," said the following in a statement on their website about the SCOTUS decision to legalize gay "marriage":

> This is a tragic day for America's children. The SCOTUS has just undermined the single greatest pro-child institution in the history of mankind: the natural family. Just as it did in the joint Roe v. Wade and Doe v. Bolton decisions, the SCOTUS has elevated and enshrined the wants of adults over the needs of children.[9]

Despite what many gay "marriage" activists say, having two mommies or two daddies does not replace God's design of one mom and one dad. God — not man or government — designed marriage for one man and one woman. From the very beginning He blessed this union, commanding, "Be fruitful and multiply" (Gen. 1:28). Homosexual couples are incapable of this as they cannot procreate like the rest of humanity usually does naturally. This, even from an evolutionary standpoint, makes the sin of homosexuality aberrant and unnatural.

Since God is the all-wise, all-knowing Creator, what He designed is obviously the only biologically feasible way for humanity to exist. It's also the only true way for us, not what sinful, fallible human beings try to make. Of course, no family is perfect. We live in a fallen world that is groaning from sin — but the creation is not at liberty to change the Creator's design for marriage and family. When we do, we are fastly approaching a head-on collision with a cultural collapse and disaster.

---

9. http://www.acpeds.org/tragic-day-for-americas-children.

I encourage you to be bold in standing on God's Word and refusing to compromise with man's ideas about what a marriage or a family should look like. Christians must unashamedly uphold the design given to us by our Creator.

My message to the president and the Supreme Court regarding gay "marriage" is this: Mr. President and members of the Supreme Court, you did not invent marriage — God did! The *Supreme Court*, ruled by the *Judge* who has ultimate and absolute authority, has already decided what marriage is:

> And He answered and said to them, "Have you not read that He who made them at the beginning 'made them male and female,' and said, 'For this reason a man shall leave his father and mother and be joined to his wife, and the two shall become one flesh'? So then, they are no longer two but one flesh" (Matt. 19:4–6).

AiG stands with others who embrace the clear and historic truth of Scripture regarding this critically important issue.

As churches, pastors, and even entire denominations cave in to compromise on homosexuality and gay "marriage," we stand resolute and unmoved, firmly rooted in God's Word which affirms,

> Forever, O LORD, Your word is settled in heaven (Ps. 119:89; NKJV).

Men and their beliefs may change, but God's Word never does. Envisioning this type of future departure from Scripture, Paul admonished pastor Timothy,

> I charge you therefore before God and the Lord Jesus Christ, who will judge the living and the dead at His appearing and His kingdom: Preach the word! Be ready in season and out of season. Convince, rebuke, exhort, with all longsuffering and teaching. For the time will come when they will not endure sound doctrine, but according to their own desires, because they have itching ears, they will heap up for themselves teachers; and they will turn their ears away from the truth, and be turned

aside to fables. But you be watchful in all things, endure afflictions, do the work of an evangelist, fulfill your ministry (2 Tim. 4:1–5; NKJV).

Peter reminds us, "They will give account to him who is ready to judge the living and the dead (1 Pet. 4:5).

Hope for the Remnant

Now, especially after this decision by the Supreme Court, many people are comparing and will compare America with Sodom and Gomorrah, two cities notorious for homosexuality that were eventually destroyed by God because of their wickedness (Gen. 19). But unlike in Sodom and Gomorrah, where God could not even find ten righteous people (Gen. 18:16–33), there is a remnant of Christians here in America who *do* base their thinking, beliefs, and behavior on God's Word. And it's a larger remnant than you may think. We meet these faithful followers of Christ every day at the Creation Museum and at conferences and other ministry events. We praise God for these faithful followers who remain true to His Word and who have not compromised themselves with man's ideas about morality.

We certainly hope that it won't reach the point where Christians and pastors are going to prison for their religious beliefs, but, realistically, with the way things are going, our precious religious freedom might just vanish in the wake of this decision by a bare majority of five justices who apparently deem themselves more knowledgeable and righteous than God on the subject of marriage. But this will only get worse if the Church doesn't wake up and return to its firm foundation of God's Word.

Despite this disappointing decision from SCOTUS that is sure to cause more challenges and redefinitions of marriage down the road, true Christians (the Remnant) need to be bold in doing our part to share the gospel — in love and without compromise — with those who desperately need it. God can use each and every one of us to reach someone with the gospel of Jesus Christ. And it's only through the gospel that we will see hearts and lives changed for eternity and eventually see change in this nation.

Sometimes I fear that even many Christians think that the solution to America's moral problems (including the legalization of gay "marriage," abortion, and so on) is a political one — to work at mainly changing the culture through legislation and sometimes litigation. I suggest that these social problems are spiritual ones — heart issues. The Bible doesn't say to go into all the world and change the culture; we are told:

> Go into all the world and proclaim the gospel to the whole creation (Mark 16:15).

> Go therefore and make disciples of all nations (Matt. 28:19).

Now as we follow this command, we are also told to

> . . . contend for the faith that was once for all delivered to the saints (Jude 3).

> . . . in your hearts honor Christ the Lord as holy, always being prepared to make a defense to anyone who asks you for a reason for the hope that is in you; yet do it with gentleness and respect (1 Pet. 3:15).

The point is, if you just try to change the culture in the sense of just working for political change, what will happen when the next generation comes through who may reject God even more, and then just change the laws back to what they want? Ultimately, any legal document, such as the U.S. Constitution, is only as good as the worldview of those interpreting it. Because of man's sinful heart, people will interpret such a document to say whatever they want it to say — which we have seen already happen in regard to abortion, the so-called "separation of church and state," and the gay "marriage" issues.

We need to be reminded that God's Word states, "For as he thinks in his heart, so is he" (Prov. 23:7; NKJV).

Hearts and minds change a culture. That's why the Scripture informs us that we are "the salt of the earth" (Matt. 5:13), but it goes on to warn us that if the salt is contaminated, it is not good for anything. We are also instructed in Mark 9:50 to "have salt in yourselves." You can't be the salt until you have salt (and you need to have uncontaminated salt).

I am not saying Christians should therefore not get involved polit-
ically — quite the opposite. What I'm saying is that Christians need to
understand that we need to be raising generations who are filled with as
much uncontaminated salt as possible. They need to be taught what they
believe and know how to defend the Christian faith. We need to raise
generations of godly people committed to the Lord Jesus Christ, who
will have a consistent Christian worldview, so when they get into positions of authority in the government, education, business, and so on,
their Christian worldview will enable them to view the legal documents
in the correct way — and then be real salt in influencing the culture.

Christians should vote in elections. By doing so, they can help be
salt and light to influence the culture for good by voting for those people
who have a consistent Christian worldview. But if we just think that all
we need to do is vote for some so-called "conservatives" (whatever that
word means these days) and it will change the culture, then the effort
will fail! We need to be concentrating on raising up hearts and minds
who will stand on God's Word so they can be the ones to influence the
culture.

Sadly, most children from our church homes have been trained by
the world, and so they have adopted a very secular worldview. Because
they've been trained by the world and therefore think like the world,
many are voting in a very anti-Christian way. Many so-called "conservatives," for instance, are voting for gay "marriage." We need people who
have an absolute basis for their worldview — based on the absolute
authority of the Word of God.

As Jeremiah warned God's people, "Thus says the LORD: 'Do not
learn the way of the Gentiles' " (Jer. 10:2; NKJV). He was telling them
they were to influence the world, not the other way round. Sadly, just
as in the times of Jeremiah, Christians have, by and large, let the world
influence generations in the Church, and now much of the Church
thinks like the world.

You cannot ultimately change a culture from the top down, when
it has changed from the foundation up. Sadly, the secular world has
understood that by capturing the hearts and minds of generations of
young people, they could change the culture from the foundation up.

Many Christians look at the consequences of this change and try to effect change from the top down! Instead, our change has happened to the foundation, so now it will be a hard, long, slow process to reverse this massive change in the culture. But again, the way to do this is for Christians to be diligent in helping change one heart at a time, little by little (starting in their homes and churches), and continue to be salt and light as best they can in a culture that has increasingly been overtaken by darkness.

We urge you to pray that God will use us — this generation of His Church — to bring revival to the United States and a return to God's Word as the foundation for our nation's thinking. And though originally written in the context of Israel and the Temple, the principle of this well-known verse still rings true:

> If my people who are called by my name humble them-selves, and pray and seek my face and turn from their wicked ways, then I will hear from heaven and will forgive their sin and heal their land (2 Chron. 7:14).

Ken Ham

Ken Ham is president and founder of Answers in Genesis and one of the most in-demand speakers in the world today. He is the author of numerous books, including co-authoring *Already Gone* and *Already Compromised*, addressing the issues of young people leaving the Church and the impact of secular concepts at Christian colleges. *Ready to Return* is the final book in this landmark series and reveals a biblically relevant path to church leaders and pastors to bring those lost back to the faith.

Ken is part of the visionary team behind the Creation Museum and now the Ark Encounter, an all-wood full-size Noah's ark being built to the historic dimensions stated in Genesis 6 (using the long cubit) in Kentucky. It will be both one of the largest "green" construction projects and timber-frame structures in the United States.

Ken is heard daily on the radio feature *Answers with Ken Ham*, broadcast on more than 850 stations, and is a frequent guest on national TV talk shows. He has appeared on Fox's *The O'Reilly Factor* and *Fox and Friends in the Morning*, CNN's *The Situation Room* with Wolf Blitzer, ABC's *Good Morning America*, the BBC, *CBS News Sunday Morning*, *NBC Nightly News*, the PBS *NewsHour* with Jim Lehrer, and many others.

Ken's emphasis is on the relevance and authority of the Book of Genesis to the life of the average Christian, and how compromise on Genesis has opened a dangerous door regarding how the culture and church view biblical authority. His 2014 creation/evolution debate with Bill Nye "The Science Guy," has been watched by an estimated 15 million people.

Britt Beemer

In 1979, Beemer founded America's Research Group, a full-service consumer behavior research and strategic marketing firm. Recognized nationally as a premier marketing strategist, he has gained wide acclaim for his work on how, when, and why consumers select their products and services. His client list represents America's top retailers, leading brands, and smaller entrepreneurial companies. His knowledge of consumer preferences increases monthly as ARG conducts thousands of new interviews.

Britt Beemer's expertise covers each phase of survey research, including questionnaire design, sample construction, and data analysis, but especially interpretation. He serves as the senior director of research at America's Research Group, where he personally reviews all research and prepares and presents each strategic marketing plan.

He holds a BA from Northwest Missouri State University and has an MA from Indiana State University. His work has been cited in the media, including the *Wall Street Journal, the New York Times, Investor's Business Daily,* CNN, Fox News, Fox Business News, and many others. He is the author of *Predatory Marketing, It Takes a Prophet to Make a Profit,* and *The Customer Rules.*

Jeff Kinley

Author and speaker Jeff Kinley has spent over three decades empowering people with vintage truth. He has written over 20 books, including the bestselling *As It Was in the Days of Noah.* Jeff holds a ThM. from Dallas Theological Seminary and speaks across the country. He and his wife live in Arkansas and have three grown sons. See jeffkinley.com for more information about his ministry.

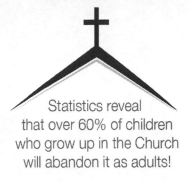
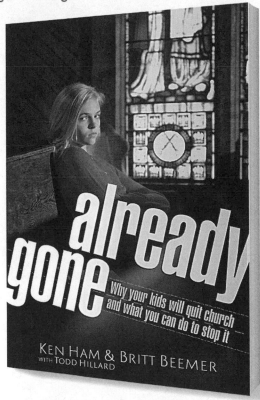

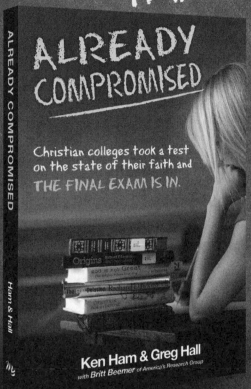